# NORMAN C. HILL

# INCREASING MANAGERIAL EFFECTIVENESS

## KEYS TO MANAGEMENT AND MOTIVATION

**ADDISON-WESLEY PUBLISHING COMPANY**
*Reading, Massachusetts • Menlo Park, California*
*London • Amsterdam • Don Mills, Ontario • Sydney*

59227

ISBN 0-201-02888-3
ABCDEFGHIJ-DO-79

# PREFACE

This book is intended to provide those who manage with a personal study guide for improving managerial effectiveness. It is also written for those who are interested in developing new managers. Each chapter focuses on some important managerial skill and describes both the basis for that skill in managerial work and some of its specific applications.

This is a practical book. It describes activities and actions that work. It is based on research into as well as observations on a variety of managerial tasks, functions, and tendencies. It is an attempt to collect and synthesize some of the more important descriptions of effective management practices. It reflects the work of many people.

Sir Isaac Newton once said, "If I have seen farther than most men, it is because I have stood on the shoulders of giants." If this book presents a clear picture of how managers can improve their effectiveness, it will be because it draws on the writings of giants who have patiently studied various aspects of managerial work. In particular, the reader will see the influence of Henry Mintzberg, whose research provided a focus for this book. Other giants are here, too, including Peter Drucker, Rensis Likert, Fritz Roethlisberger, and Douglas MacGregor.

In addition to these, three others have had a profound influence on me, personally as well as professionally. Gene Dalton first encouraged me to write this book, and I continue to appreciate his friendship. J. B. Ritchie taught me to look for the unintended consequences of what appeared on the surface to be good answers to tough problems. And Bill Dyer's clear writing and plain talk have provided valuable models to emulate.

I have had the opportunity to work as a consultant to several organizations. Mel Bennett, a good friend, first started me in this direction, providing the opportunity to gain some valuable experience. Several people here at Exxon have continued that practice. Don Cherry, in particular, has opened a number of doors for me. So, too, have Bill Faison, Dan Muschalik, and Thornton Larimer.

An author's work must stand on its own merits, and I hope that mine does. This book is based on my own observations and research and was written on my own time. It is not intended to reflect the philosophy of Exxon or of its management staff; I alone am responsible for the contents. However, the contributions of many are represented here. Some of these contributions are acknowledged in the references, in which I have sought to give proper attribution wherever possible. The contributions of others, such as my wife, family, and friends, are more difficult to properly identify. The influence of Raelene, Ryan and other family members has been significant. I thank Norman Guess at Dartnell for permission to include material I had previously written for him. I am also grateful to Charles Peers at Addison-Wesley for his help and support.

Finally, I hope that you who read this book benefit as much from reading it as I did from writing it.

*Houston, Texas*                                                    N. C. H.
*November 1978*

# CONTENTS

# CHAPTER I
# WHAT DO
# MANAGERS DO?

Ask managers what they do and the replies will probably be something like "plan, organize, direct and control." But *observe* what these same managers do and it may be difficult to see how these four words are adequate. As Canadian management professor Henry Mintzberg has noted, among others, these four words merely seem to describe certain vague objectives of management and say very little about what managers actually do.[1]

Somehow, in the rush to automate production, to use computer and behavioral sciences in industry, and to apply the latest technological processes, the managers—those people in charge of an organizational unit—have been overlooked. Improved organizational procedures in various areas have simply not supplied an adequate answer to the essential question of what managers do. Without such an answer, how can management be taught? How can managers plan self-development activities to improve their effectiveness? How can the practice of management be improved?

There are some very compelling reasons for exploring these questions. Their answers provide a guide to the ways in which people occupying managerial positions can perform effectively. By knowing what managers are supposed to do, those people can think about their own work and how they do it. They can assess how well they are performing managerial activities and make any necessary adjustments in time allocations or in work practices. Such a perspective is also useful in planning the future and considering the things necessary for fully developing their potential.

It is possible for managers to be very busy and still not be very effective. They may be busy doing things that do not count very much. Moreover, unless managers have a clear conception of the basic activities they are supposed to perform, they will not be able to make plans or establish priorities for self-improvement. Like carpenters, managers must have a variety of tools in the tool kit and know both *when* and *how* to use each one. Otherwise, as the late Abraham Maslow purportedly said, "if you only have one tool and it's a hammer, then you tend to treat everything as if it were a nail."

The lack of a clear picture among many managers of what constitutes managerial work limits their effectiveness. Without a model or a standard with which to compare themselves, how can they know how well they are doing? Managers need to know what truly represents managerial work in order to be able to turn the common characteristics of their jobs into unique individual applications.

## CHARACTERISTICS OF MANAGERIAL WORK

There are two conflicting views on how managers prefer to work. One view maintains that managers are careful, systematic planners who like to make decisions in a relaxed and reflective manner. In addition, this perspective suggests that good managers, like good music conductors, carefully coordinate a variety of activities without actively particpating in any of them.

The other view of managerial work suggests that it is not as orderly and predictable as the first view would imply. Rather, managerial activities are generally fragmented, brief, and thought through on the run. In addition, managers must handle boundary relationships well in order to link their units to others within the organization as well as to society at large. Finally, managers must be involved enough in day-to-day operations, so that their fingers are on the pulse of the unit, and they can provide direction or support as needed.

Study and research suggest that, although managers are a blend of both these views, the latter position is the more accurate description of managerial work. Managers must exercise judgment and make decisions with incomplete information on a regular basis. It is a fact of managerial life. They cannot plan one year or one month in advance except in very general terms. They must work through problems as they arise and in many cases must decide on an immediate course of action. There are no rigid rules and few lock step procedures that can realistically apply in every case. Unlike those who simply observe, managers must act. This imperative requires that managers develop a few "rules of thumb" in addition to relying on their own hunches, intuition, and experience in performing their daily work.

Groups of management researchers working independently at universities and various organizations across the country have sought to go beyond this basic description and to identify the effect of various managerial approaches on employee output and morale. A composite of their findings (the following table) is most interesting. Clearly, there are some things that effective managers do differently from their less-effective counterparts.[2]

## Have high concern for people and productivity

One of the most consistent findings from research on managerial work is that effective managers are concerned with both people and productivity. This is a critical balance. If employees feel that

## A Comparison of Managerial Styles

| Characteristics of Managers Whose Units are High in Employee Output and Morale | Characteristics of Managers Whose Units are Low in Employee Output and Morale |
|---|---|
| 1. Have high concern for people and productivity. | 1. Have high concern for productivity only. |
| 2. Spend time managing. | 2. Spend time on own work. |
| 3. Use a general style. | 3. Use a close or punitive style. |
| 4. Build group pride. | 4. Work only one-to-one with subordinates. |
| 5. Keep people informed. | 5. Restrict information given to employees. |
| 6. Allow employees to influence them. | 6. Are not open to others' ideas. |
| 7. Take pressure off in a crisis. | 7. Apply pressure in a crisis. |
| 8. Have influence upward. | 8. Make promises about what they will do that are often broken or ignored. |
| 9. Minimize status distinctions. | 9. Emphasize status distinctions. |
| 10. Are willing to do detail work. | 10. Remain aloof from day-to-day operations. |

they are regarded simply as pairs of hands and that they are expendable, they will not feel any commitment towards organizational goals. This does not imply that a "country club" style of managing is best. Clearly, it is not. People work best with standards and performance expectations that stretch their capacities. Effective managers are able to communicate by the things they *do*—not by the slogans they repeat—that they are equally concerned about people and productivity and expect others to be similarly concerned.

There is in addition some good evidence suggesting that work-centered managers, who view people merely as instruments in the production process engage in actions that are ultimately self-defeating. The more they try to control everything that happens and to boost output, the more people feel resentful and try to resist the pressure they impose. This often triggers a cycle of more pressure and more resistance, which diverts everyone's efforts away from the goals they really want.

## Spend time managing

Another common characteristic of effective managers is that they spend most of their time managing. That is, they spend most of their time identifying opportunities for improvement, locating problems, training subordinates, developing contacts with others in the organization, working through interunit differences, and the like. They see themselves at the center of a large informational, interpersonal, and decisional network that demands continual attention and constant scrutiny. Moreover, these networks are dynamic and change from week to week. Managing is something effective managers see as a full-time job.

Ineffective managers, however, tend to view managerial activities as requiring only a small portion of their time. Instead, they channel their efforts into record keeping and their own technical work. (This is especially true of people with a background in engineering.) Ineffective managers are unprepared for or uncomfortable with managerial work and so they spend little time actually doing it.

## Use a general style

Some people might be surprised to learn that effective managers do not spend a significantly larger portion of time with their employees than do ineffective managers, but it is true. Effective managers have fewer contacts with subordinates, but they spend more time during each individual visit than ineffective managers usually do. Research by management professor Quentin Ponder has demonstrated that effective managers engage in discussions with their subordinates about the overall scope and purpose of a work assignment, so the employees are able to proceed on their own to fill the requirements of the project.[3]

Ineffective managers interact with subordinates in a very different way. They give instructions for only a portion of a project and will generally drop by only to check on their subordinates' progress with work assignments. People who work for such managers frequently report that the only time they see their bosses is when they are checking up on them or reprimanding them.

William Dyer, a Brigham Young University management professor, suggests that it is easy to tell if managers use a general style or one that is close and punitive. Dyer does this by posing the following kind of question to managers' subordinates:

> Suppose you get a call from your boss. What's your reaction? Is it, "Oh, good. I always look forward to talking to him." Or do you instead stiffen and say, "Uh, oh. What's he going to get on me for now?"

The difference in the manner and content of managers' instructions to subordinates plays a powerful part in the managers' effectiveness.

### Build group pride

Another characteristic of effective managers is that they work with their employees in groups or subgroups on a regular basis. They allow the people they supervise to talk with each other, share ideas, and establish some common perspectives. Such managers realize that if "espirit de corps" is going to be developed in a unit, then employees must be able to occasionally work as a unit. Staff meetings where problems are worked on as a group or where everyone contributes to future goals must also be held to achieve this objective. In order to identify with each other and have a sense of group pride, employees must do some work together.

Ineffective managers make no such attempt to bring all of their people together to work common problems. Instead, they prefer to work one-to-one and to keep the work of subordinates separated. Although such an orientation increases control over subordinates, it also decreases employee motivation and job satisfaction.

## Keep people informed

People just seem to want to know what is going on around them. If some change is going to affect their work, they want as much advance notice of it as their managers can supply. It is a sign of concern and respect for others, and good managers take deliberate steps to keep them informed. In fact, Harvard psychologist David McClelland, who has done extensive research on the achievement motivation of people, has found that it makes a real difference in their performance if people are given regular feedback and kept informed about what's happening in the organization that affects their workday lives.[4]

When information is not shared with employees on matters that affect them, it is not unusual for them to feel that they are being taken advantage of or even cheated. "Why weren't we informed?" they may think or ask. "Aren't we trusted or is it that we just don't count for very much around here?" Ineffective managers do not take the time or may not feel the need to share information freely with employees. The result is that such managers get less done because the people they supervise are less cooperative and more dissatisfied than employees who report to managers who believe in keeping their people informed.

## Allow employees to influence them

Effective managers are aware of their own limitations and therefore seek information and advice from others. They are open to good information, whatever the source. Employees who work for such managers are often able to influence them because the managers are secure in their own self-evaluations. Their levels of self-esteem are high, so they feel neither threatened nor insecure when employees come up with good ideas for doing things differently.

Ineffective managers, however, get few new ideas from employees because they have established a record of disregarding employee suggestions. Such managers may believe that the reason employees do no more than they are told is because they are lazy or indolent. However, in some situations managers' actions may be limiting employee motivation and commitment. Authoritarian managers cause people to be cautious about doing more than they are specifically told to do because of the reprimands frequently delivered.

## Take pressure off in a crisis

Crises are inevitable in managerial work. Things do not always go exactly as they should. How do managers handle a situation in which a deadline must be met or an error committed by a subordinate must be corrected? Effective managers respond to such situations by taking some of the pressure off others and encouraging them to do their best. This does not mean that they overlook errors or the root cause of a crisis. Rather they get the work out first and analyze the performance problem after the storm has passed.

In a crisis, ineffective managers apply more pressure rather than remove any of it. They continue to reiterate the importance of a deadline or the cause of an error. Consequently, people feel more stress and are less likely to perform at their best. Under such conditions, additional mistakes are likely to occur.

## Have influence upward

The ability to influence their own bosses' decisions is an essential characteristic of effective managers. They must be skilled as subordinates as well as proficient as supervisors. In nearly every work situation there are cases in which employees want the managers to take action on their concerns or suggestions. Although they may not expect the managers to act in response to every complaint or suggestion, if the managers never take action on such matters, employees will probably come to believe that they have no power.

Managers whose power is limited often adopt a risky strategy. When they are approached by subordinates to take action on some matter, they may make promises about what they are going to do and how they are going to influence others.

The manager may, however, have no intention of really advocating the workers' position and may make a promise simply to pacify the subordinates. They assume that in a day or two the matter will be completely forgotten. Subordinates, however, rarely forget and such managers soon get a reputation for being unable to deliver on their promises.

## Minimize status differences

Status symbols are an ubiquitous part of managerial work. The real question is: Do managers minimize or emphasize status distinctions between themselves and others? There is an important reason for minimizing these distinctions. If the status differences are very great between these two adjoining work levels, communication and cooperation will break down.

Effective organizational functioning requires the free flow of information between and among various organizational units. People must feel comfortable to speak up and say what they think. Otherwise, employees will pass on to managers only those things they think the managers want to hear. If managers emphasize status distinctions, they will be less likely to get the information they need and the cooperation they value. The assumption that employees will respect managers who emphasize status distinctions and who are careful not to meet them on an equal plane is simply erroneous.

## Are willing to do detail work

Some management writers have compared managers to orchestra conductors, "by whose efforts, vision and leadership individual instrumental parts that are so much noise by themselves become the living whole of music."[5] One such poetic writer has even cautioned managers about getting too involved in day-to-day operations. Unfortunately, such advice about what managers should do does not compare with what effective managers actually do.

Managers must walk a fine line between doing managerial and technical work. They must know the work of each person they supervise well enough to help out with tough problems, but they must also know the character of each employee well enough to know when to let them struggle. The manager who responds to requests for help from subordinates and is able to give it, or who volunteers help that is desired but not asked for, is typically described by employees as "someone you can talk to, someone who listens and understands." Effective managers are involved enough in the work of each person they supervise to know what aid to give when help is needed and where time can be spent profitably when it is not. This differentiates those who manage from both those who meddle and those who orchestrate.

## MANAGERIAL FUNCTIONS

All managers are vested with formal authority to do certain things in an organizational unit. This authority prescribes some formal relationships between the managers and others and provides them with access to certain kinds of information. Such authority also provides for certain decisions to be made by the managers. These three basic aspects of managerial work—informational functions, interpersonal functions, and decisional functions—all require the proper use of appropriate skills if the managers are to be effective. It is not enough to know what to do, managers must know *how* to do the work required of them.

## THE INFORMATIONAL FUNCTION

Managers are the nerve centers of an organizational unit. They do not leave meetings or hang up the telephone in order to get back to work. In large measure, communication is their work. However, getting and giving information in order to communicate take effort and commitment. They also require the use of some important skills.

In many organizations, managers do not suffer from a lack of information per se. In fact, in some instances they have more information than they need to take action on various matters—they work under an "information overload." However, much of this information may be wrong or without specific enough categories, and therefore of little real value. For instance, financial data may be distributed throughout the organization in aggregate form only, or safety reports may contain only numerical averages. In either case, managers need more specific, and more focused information in order to take appropriate action on these matters.

Effective managers get their most useful information from talking with people—with lots of people, and often. Formal information systems provide managers only with past data. Consequently, they must get out of their offices and talk to others in order to get current information. To do this, managers need to develop skills in three important areas. First, they need skills to develop interpersonal relations so that they can get raw, unedited information from the people with whom they work. Second, they need to know how to exchange information and sort out priorities with employees and others in a group setting. Third, they need to be able to monitor activities in such a way that employees feel supervised, not "snoopervised." How well and in what manner managers develop skills in these three areas largely determines their effectiveness in the informational aspects of managerial work.

## THE INTERPERSONAL FUNCTION

Managers work with other people to solve problems. To do this effectively, they must be able to influence what and how other people do things. This is not easy because people have different personalities and different backgrounds; the only apparent similarity characterizing a particular group of employees may be the fact that they all work at the same place. This is why, to be effective, managers must always adapt their behavior to take into account the expectations, values, and perceptions of the people with whom they are interacting. This applies to all their relationships—with peers, subordinates, and superiors.

People are different, and the differences must be given more acknowledgement than mere lip service. In fact, such differences between and among employees can be a major source of problems if they are not managed well. Managers need to develop skills in how to manage these differences and to have them work to their advantage. They must also learn how to work with employees in ways that challenge them and stretch their productive capacities to the limit of their abilities. To do this, managers must go beyond the slogan of "people are our most important resource" to the development of effective interpersonal skills.

## THE DECISIONAL FUNCTION

Managers make decisions, lots of them, every day. Decisions are constantly being made at various levels of an organization all of the time. Decision making is an integral part of managerial work. However, it is not always done wisely or well because it is viewed as a rational process, in which choices are made simply on the basis of available facts. Although the decisional aspects of managerial work certainly include making choices on that basis, it is not limited to this.

Decision making is a *social* process as well as a rational process, and it requires managers to not just solve problems but also to find them. To make effective decisions, managers must be aware of the various components of the problems they face. This is not easy because the pace and scope of the work often prevents them from planning a course of action and then pursuing it. Still, they can control their activities through the effort of scheduling their time.

Time is an important managerial resource. Where managers decide to spend their time dramatically affects their performance. The schedule may very well dictate which decisions they will make and which decisions will be made by someone else and submitted to them for approval. In some situations, it is very desirable for other people, who may have better information, to make the decisions and pass them on for approval. In other situations, it is not. *How* managers make such decisions may, in fact, be some of the more important decisions they make.

There are some important managerial skills related to these three managerial functions. Their proper development and application determine managerial effectiveness. Ten characteristics of effective managers have been briefly explored in this chapter.

They describe what effective managers do. However, there is a big difference in knowing *what* to do and knowing *how* to do it.

Each of the next nine chapters describe some specific "how to's" for effective managerial behavior. They illustrate some of the things many managers have found useful, practical, and productive. The techniques and tools offered in these chapters are not, however, surefire remedies. Instead, they are guides that a number of managers in a variety of diverse situations have applied to their own jobs.

## SUMMARY

The managers of today's organizations, whether business enterprises, government agencies, or educational institutions, are confronted by a different set of circumstances than were their predecessors 20 or 30 years ago. A highly educated work force, a technologically complex society, and a constantly changing world are but a few of the differences that past administrators would notice as being common concerns faced by today's managers.

It is a different world, requiring a different kind of manager in order to operate effectively. It requires managers who will not be overrun by external pressures or demands, who are comfortable in dealing with people in general as well as with the problem employee down the hall. It requires managers who are willing to study their position and decide how they are going to be effective in it.

Effectiveness does not just happen. It takes effort. It also takes effort in the right direction. A manager must be more than busy. A manager can be very busy turning out reports or churning through paperwork without being effective; being effective is being busy doing the right things. Finding out what those right things are is a major managerial responsibility. It is not an easy task, but there are no alternatives for today's manager.

## REFERENCES

1.  Henry Mintzberg, *The Nature of Managerial Work*. New York: Harper & Row, 1973.
2.  See, for instance, Robert R. Blake and Jane S. Mouton, *The Managerial Grid*. Houston: Gulf Publishing, 1964; Alfred J. Marrow, David G. Bowers and

Stanley Seashore, *Management by Participation*. New York: Harper & Row, 1967; Rensis Likert, *The Human Organization*. New York: McGraw-Hill, 1967; Thomas Burns and G. M. Stalker, *The Management of Innovation*. London: Tavistock, 1961; and William F. Whyte, *Organizational Behavior: Theory and Application*. Homewood, Ill.: Irwin-Dorsey, 1969.

3.  "The Effective Manufacturing Foreman," in Edward Yound, ed., *Industrial Relations Research Association Proceedings*. Madison, Wis.: IRRA, 1957, pp. 41–54.

4.  David C. McClelland, *The Achieving Society*. New York: The Free Press, 1967.

5.  Leonard R. Sayles, *Managerial Behavior*. New York: McGraw-Hill, 1964, p. 162.

# PART I
# THE INFORMATIONAL
# FUNCTION

# CHAPTER 2
# IMPROVING
# COMMUNICATION SKILLS

It has been said that men and women are the only creatures on earth who can talk themselves into trouble. In fact, after 30 or 40 years of practice, some people even become pretty good at it. Communication problems are so commonplace, however, that the fault is probably not in people as much as in the processes they use. Perhaps we have all taken our ability to communicate with each other for granted, and what we have assumed to be a simple, natural process is much more complex than most of us suppose.

All managers have a common objective in communicating. They are attempting to influence the way things happen through what they do and say. Unfortunately, some managers still believe that all they have to do to influence others is to give an order or issue a directive. People, however, do not do things simply because they are told to do them; they do things because they have reasons for doing them. Most people expect to know the reasons for an assignment or task, and they perform better when they have a clear understanding of both what is expected and why it is required.

Since communication is so central to a manager's job, understanding how to communicate in ways that motivate people and get work done is an important skill to learn. This involves more than being persuasive and logical. Although people do things because they have reasons, their reasons may not always be rational. Understanding the nonrational reasons for the way people act can increase a manager's effectiveness in ways that pay dividends in dollars and cents.

To many people, communication is the process whereby one person gets someone else to agree with his ideas, opinions, facts, or information. If there is a communication problem such people assume that it is due to a lack of persuasion, logical thinking, or the properly chosen words. However, another possibly more appropriate way to regard communication problems is as evidence of a breakdown in the relationship between the two people who are talking. Thus, communication problems do not result because one person is not clear enough in self-expression, but because of a misevaluation between the two parties of what is actually taking place.

Suppose, for instance, a manager calls an employee into the office and says, "I think you could do some things differently in your job that would help you be more effective." If the employee listens and does things differently, is it because the boss presented the ideas lucidly or is it because the employee respects the boss's authority and knowledge? It is difficult to pinpoint an exact reason for the employee's making the changes, but it is certain that there were more dynamics involved than just the actual exchange. Perhaps, then, a useful way to study and improve interpersonal communication is to examine the road blocks that prevent, and the road signs that facilitate, understanding.

## COMMUNICATION ROAD BLOCKS

"It takes two to speak truth," the early American naturalist Henry David Thoreau once said, "one to speak and another to hear." Communication, in fact, occurs only when there is mutual understanding. People understanding people, however, is probably one of the foremost problems in management today. A newspaper account of how managers in one company reacted to the court-imposed changes regarding mandatory retirement illustrates the difficulty some managers have in communicating with employees, especially those with problems.

> The middle managers were upset. It looked like their company was going to lose mandatory retirement for 65-year-olds and they didn't like that at all. Mandatory retirement, they said, was neat; no muss, no fuss. It cleaned out the deadwood and put a deadline on the work life of employees.
>
> The workers they were talking about are familiar. There's some in every office. The incompetent or the embittered, the stumbler or the coaster. They can be found up and down the age ladder. Many offices develop elaborate dynamics to deal with such people problems—by any means except the direct and personal ones. Only the best bosses can handle these human situations that require understanding and negotiation.[1]

While comfortable with their power over things, many managers are uncomfortable with their power over people, and least comfortable dealing with them in person. Managers at all levels in an organization need a clearer understanding of the factors that hinder and those that help communication in a variety of interpersonal situations. This guide will partially respond to that need.

## BARRIER: THE TENDENCY TO EVALUATE

Carl Rogers, a pioneer in the development of interpersonal communication methods, maintains that a major barrier to communication effectiveness is "our very natural tendency to judge, to evaluate, to approve, or to disapprove the statements of another person or group." Rogers maintains that this tendency to evaluate inhibits communication because it increases combativeness and decreases mutual understanding.[2]

Let's examine this tendency and its effects with some examples. Suppose one employee approaches a second employee in the department and says "I don't think there's much of a future in this place." How will the second employee respond? Almost invariably the reply will express either approval or disapproval. Either the second employee will respond, "I've thought that way myself for some time now" or "Oh, I think there is a lot of opportunity here." In either case, the second employee is evaluating the initial remark from an individual point of view, or frame of reference. Why does that inhibit communication? Because it tends to create a win-lose situation, where some people are "right" and others are "wrong." Such an attitude creates chasms that divide people rather than bridges that unite them. Since communication is a process for achieving mutal understanding, it is evident that this common tendency to judge and evaluate hinders effective interpersonal relations.

An extension of this tendency to evaluate is an inclination to judge a source as either acceptable or unacceptable and on that basis decide on a position or a course of action. William H. Whyte, a former editor of *Fortune* magazine, demonstrated the pervasiveness of this inclination with a little experiment. First, he clipped from a union publication a cartoon illustrating "The Four Goals of Labor." Then he pasted it on a bulletin board with a caption indicating that the source was the National Association of Manufacturers. As union members passed by the bulletin board and read the clipping, they were overwhelmingly critical of it as an unfair and biased representation of labor's goals. Having accepted the source as antilabor, they automatically drew the obvious conclusion that the message was also antilabor.[3]

These tendencies to evaluate are no less prevalent among managers than among union members. To decide quickly rather than to seek understanding diligently appears to be a general characteristic of people. Moreover, merely wanting to understand and be understood by others is insufficient; the cultivation of skills in active listening is also essential.

## GATEWAY: ACTIVE LISTENING

Real communication occurs when this tendency to make a quick evaluation is avoided and listening for understanding is practiced. This doesn't mean that managers don't eventually evaluate information they have gained in a conversation, but it does mean that they consider whether the time is appropriate to air their own opinions. Initially, what a manager needs to do when others in the organization are expressing their ideas or opinions is to try and understand *their* feelings and *their* point of view.

People who work together in an organization can do so more cooperatively by seeking to understand one another and each other's proposals before launching into evaluation. Too often in staff meetings or on other occasions, the turmoil of partisanship prevents the communication of either ideas or respect. In their haste to get to a solution, managers in such situations may fail to carefully examine the full scope of the problem. The economic significance of these failures to listen to full definitions of problems as well as all feasible alternatives is obvious.

Listening for understanding means much more than simply hearing words and knowing their meaning. The effort required to listen well has been described by Ralph Nichols, a management consultant, who has written that white-collar workers devote at least 40% of their workday to listening. Apparently, 40% of their salary is paid to them for their listening. He says that tests of listening comprehension have shown that, without training, these employees listen at only 30% efficiency. It seems, therefore, that listening is more than just hearing.

This is important to realize and can be illustrated quite easily. Suppose, for instance, that a manager is looking for information in an open drawer in a filing cabinet. Along comes a secretary familiar with the filing system, who asks, "Looking for something?"

Would the manager take the words literally? If so, the response might be quite caustic, along the lines of "Anyone who wasn't blind could see that that's the case." However, the literal meaning of the words will probably be ignored, and instead their *intention* would evoke a response such as, "Whew, am I glad to see you!"

The secretary, of course, did not intend to have the words taken literally either. The probable intention was to say something like this: "I see that you are having some difficulty, and I would like to help you if I can. But you may want to find whatever you're looking for yourself and so view me as an intruder. So, if you want me to help, just tell me."

In listening well, then, never worry about what the words mean to you; instead, try to determine what the words mean to the speaker. This means that merely *assuming* to know what the speaker intends is not enough. If there is doubt, the listener must ask and clarify. In this sense, a statement made by George Bernard Shaw becomes extremely provocative. "The only man I know," he said, "who behaves sensibly is my tailor; he takes my measure anew each time he sees me, whilst all the rest go on with their old measurements, and expect me to fit them." This partially explains why communications break down and what can be done about it. An individual can seek to understand and clarify before evaluating instead of assuming that the words are "perfectly clear."

There are some specific tools a manager can use to avoid the tendency to make a quick evaluation. As a group, these tools are called "active listening" because they allow the receiver to actively participate in the communication process.[4] Let's examine some of the active listening tools and see how a manager might use them to improve interpersonal communication effectiveness.

### Paraphrasing

One active listening tool is paraphrasing. Paraphrasing occurs when managers restate in their own words what they believe another person has just said. This ensures the understanding of the *intent* as well as of the individual words of the speaker. It is a solution to the feeling expressed by this oft-repeated phrase: "I know you believe you understand what you think I said, but I am not sure you realize that what you heard is not what I meant."

Paraphrasing is not parroting. Rather, it is restating the intent of another person's ideas or feelings. Some phrases to use in paraphrasing include the following:

- "What I hear you saying is . . ."
- "Sounds like you feel . . ."

- "You believe that . . ."
- "Are you saying that . . ."
- "What happened was . . ."
- "You're concerned that . . ."

These are trigger phrases that can get speakers to clarify the original intent or express their feelings more completely. Just imagine what would happen if this tool were used regularly in everyday business activities. Frequently heard phrases such as "How did she get that from what I said?" and "I thought I told you not to . . ." would certainly be spoken less often and may even disappear altogether.

### "Door openers"

Another active listening technique that can promote better interpersonal communication is termed "door openers." This is a tool that can get someone else to say more about a problem or a frustrating experience. One of the common barriers to organizational improvement in many situations is the existence of rules or policies that were formed for a particular reason that is no longer valid. However, because these rules and policies are still in force, they prevent improvement in performance and effectiveness. They create problems that are uncovered only when a manager takes the time to listen to an employee who has a legitimate concern. Using "door openers" is a technique for getting someone else to say more about a troubling situation. Some door openers include:

- "Uh-huh."
- "Really."
- "I see."
- "Oh."
- "How's that."
- "Interesting."

They encourage communication because they encourage another person to say more. Too often managers assume that they must have an answer to every question or defend the status quo whenever an employee describes a problem. In turn, employees feel that there is no point in talking with these managers because they never listen, they simply reply with a pat answer.

Sometimes people just want and need to be heard. They want to blow off steam. Much of human communication asks for contact as much as content. Thus phrases such as "You have no reason to feel that way" or "If you'd look at things from my position once in a while" or "Everybody knows that . . ." prevent communication rather than facilitate it.

Using door openers can improve communication and understanding, as an experiment at a midwestern university demonstrates. A psychology professor indicated to his students at the beginning of the semester that each of them would be required to make personal visits to patients at the terminally ill ward of the local hospital once a week. They could stay as long as they wanted and talk about any subject they wished. The professor had previously obtained permission to install under each bed tape recorders that could be activated by the patient. He had also instructed the patients to avoid giving advice or moralizing when the students told them about personal problems. Instead, patients were to respond with a door opener.

At the end of the semester, the professor had made a very interesting discovery. He found that the students really began to explore the nature of their personal problems whenever the patients answered with several door openers in succession. The students described their feelings completely and freely once they were assured that they would not be judged or lectured. Moreover, the students indicated at the semester's end that they had obtained a lot of valuable counseling and information from the patients, although the tape recordings revealed that the patients had actually provided very little substantive input.[5]

These two techniques of paraphrasing and using door openers illustrate what active listening is all about. It is more than simply understanding the words that another person has spoken: It is understanding the intent and feelings the words represent.

## BARRIER: EMPHASIZING AUTHORITY

One barrier that inhibits interpersonal communication effectiveness in many organizational situations is the difference in authority levels between managers and employees. Managers may not wish this variance to affect relationships with employees, but it will unless steps are taken to minimize it. Many employees are hesitant to pass along unfavorable information to managers because of their concern that it might not be well received, an avowed "open door" policy notwithstanding. In some organizations accurate information is not rewarded and is therefore not easily given. Like the ancient Greeks who decapitated the "bearer of bad news," some managers are more likely to punish than to reward employees who identify the causes of various problems. Consequently, employees tell managers what they want to hear instead of what they should hear.

In face-to-face situations, a message is communicated by more than just words. Managers, knowingly or unknowingly, utilize a variety of nonverbal methods to either minimize or emphasize their authority. Managers can nonverbally emphasize authority and thereby inhibit interpersonal communication in the following ways:

- by remaining seated behind their desks while talking to an employee;
- by staring out the window or at the ceiling while the employee is talking,
- by allowing long stretches of silence in a conversation;
- by changing the subject for no apparent reason;
- by giving the employee little or no feedback on any of the ideas or information being passed along.

## GATEWAY: MINIMIZING STATUS DIFFERENCES

By virtue of authority, managers are at the apex of an information network. Ironically, this very position can prevent the efficient flow of information to and from employees. Somehow managers must find out which kinds of information are not readily passed along and then act on it. There are two important habits that can be developed to aid in performing this function well. These are deemphasizing status differences in everyday working relations and eliminating status barriers in one-to-one discussions.

There is an oft-repeated saying that a manager's job is to direct the activities of others and to avoid doing their work. In addition, it is believed that in order to maintain employee respect and to safeguard their authority, managers should not become too friendly with the people who report to them. This advice seems to follow the "familiarity breeds contempt" adage.

The observation of what effective managers do, however, does not support this notion. In an egalitarian society, in which people believe they are "just as good as anyone else," a manager who emphasizes status differences will be deeply resented by employees. This does not mean that all status symbols should be eliminated; in most organizations, status differences are needed to help organize people's relationships to each other. Rather, managers should refrain from emphasizing status differences and attempt to get to know well the people in their employ. As a result, the employees will have confidence in the managers' judgment and respect for their position.

Managers cannot be simply "one of the gang," however. Moreover, if they become too close to one person or group, they may be accused of playing favorites. Yet, it is quite possible and very important to establish good informal relations with employees. Without such a relationship, most employees will not feel comfortable in passing along sensitive information to their managers.

One way to develop this relationship is for the managers to take the time to periodically talk with each employee about how things are going generally. By doing so, managers nonverbally communicate their interest in the employee as a person and their accessibility as a source of help. If, in such discussions, managers can be sounding boards without taking responsibility for solving any problems the employee discusses, they will be viewed as people who let workers take initiative without abandoning them. This will, as well, communicate to employees that here are managers who use authority for improvement, not for punishment.

A second habit that managers can develop in order to effectively get and appropriately give information is that of eliminating status barriers in discussions with employees. Eaton Industries, an automotive manufacturing company, has instituted what they call "an open floor policy" to achieve this objective. At Eaton, managers are encouraged to make appointments and meet with supervisors and other employees in the supervisor's office or the employees' work area. They are also encouraged to treat each employee with respect by giving that employee their full attention during their discussion. These have been small prices to pay for the benefits reaped, according to Eaton's managers.[6]

## BARRIER: EVALUATIVE FEEDBACK

Only the best managers can handle the difficult human situations that call for understanding and negotiation. Others shy away from confronting the performance problems of their employees; in some offices, conspiracies can even develop to delicately avoid "people problems." These managers may have genuinely tried to talk with problem employees about their deficiencies, only to have been rebuffed. This hypothetical vignette describes an all-too-frequent attempt by managers to give employees performance feedback.

Manager:  Look, Walt, how many times do I have to tell you not to send in a report that's incomplete. Now take it back and rework it until you've finished.

Employee:  Wait a minute, Carol, I've got a million things to do around here. I can't read your mind. How do I know what you want?

The manager may walk away from this situation thinking "Walt can't take suggestions without getting mad," while the employee may walk away muttering "Carol never explains what she wants and then criticizes when things aren't done the 'right' way." Perhaps both are right. Even though the manager may have had good intentions, the results she wanted to achieve never materialized because of her methods, and her "suggestions" seemed to Walt to be arbitrary instead of helpful.

Many times, essentially positive intentions of being helpful and constructive fail to be accurately translated into actions because of a lack of interpersonal skills. As a result, instead of yielding more productive and satisfied employees, managers' efforts to improve things produce only discontent and dissatisfaction. Why? Because they use evaluative feedback methods. Such methods, the "if-you-know-what's-good-for-you" kind, are bound to produce resentment rather than commitment, regardless of a manager's intentions. What a manager actually says or intends is less important in interpersonal matters than what an employee hears. What can managers do, then, to communicate their intentions more completely, especially in situations where they are trying to correct a performance problem? Plenty.

## GATEWAY: DESCRIPTIVE FEEDBACK

People need to know what is expected of them if they are to perform adequately. They also want to know when they are not performing properly, but they want to know in a way that does not force them to swallow their pride or lose their self-respect. Employees need to be told in an acceptable manner if they are not performing well. Otherwise, they will be resentful of any feedback a manager may give regarding their job performance.

One manner for giving feedback to employees that is generally acceptable to people is known as an "I message."[7] "I messages" are an effective communication tool because they simply inform employees of the consequences of their actions rather than judge the actions or motives. There is even a formula for sending an "I message":

I _____ (feeling) when you _____ (behavior) because it _____ (impact).

To deal with unproductive behavior, all a manager needs to do is fill in the blanks. For instance, in dealing with an employee who has had a series of absences due to personal emergencies in recent months, the manager could send the following "I message":

> I am troubled (feeling) by the seven absences you have had in the last six months (behavior) because it has created a burden on others who have had to do your work as well as their own (consequence). I want you to know that when you miss work it affects all of us.

This formula can be used as a guide for confronting unacceptable behavior in a variety of situations. This is particularly true if the manager focuses on understanding the behavior of the employee and on sharing information instead of on attempting to judge personality traits or give advice.

On the other hand, managers may desire feedback on how their employees view them. Such sensitive information is not easily offered but can be extremely valuable. A manager can do five things to encourage feedback:

1. affirm that it is wanted;
2. identify specific areas in which feedback is needed;
3. set aside time for planned feedback sessions;
4. use silence to encourage the flow of information at feedback sessions;
5. reward people for good information, even if it is unpleasant.

Getting and giving feedback are valuable skills that every effective manager practices. Several methods are appropriate for stimulating such feedback, including one-to-one discussion, group meetings, and casual conversations. Feedback is such an integral part of the management process that every manager should develop methods for getting and giving useful feedback.

## SUMMARY

Research findings from a variety of sources show that open communication generally results in improved morale and productivity. From this research, one point is clear: the fact that improvement in communication depends less on investments in mass media than on good work relations between managers and employees. In this context, it is important that managers point out the meeting ground where the interests of both groups merge. Employees must see how they benefit concretely from commitment to and involvement in their work. They must see where and how they can contribute in specific ways, not just in general terms. How managers work on this objective can help determine whether they succeed or fail. Their actions do speak louder than their words. Moreover, managers should always remember that, in the final analysis, what counts is not what people are told but what they accept.

A manager should continually be asking such questions as "What do you mean?" "How do you know?" "What differences does it make?" These questions sound simple, but people in organizations often fail to ask them or to seek their answers. Often managers will assume they understand another person's position when, in fact, they do not. They may fail to clarify what they think they've heard, and the misunderstanding that results is astonishing. For some people such misunderstanding is beneficial, reports semanticist S. I. Hayakawa. "You cannot be respected as a scholar," Hayakawa notes, "if people understand what you say." For managers, however, this position is inadvisable.

There are four basic realities that people interested in improving interpersonal communications must recognize if they are to enhance understanding.

1. Meanings are in people, not in the words they use. It is less important to ask "What does that word mean?" than "What do you mean?" Managers who are unaware of this fact often end up saying to themselves, after an assignment has been handled badly, "But I told them how to do it correctly."

2. People tend to pass information along to a manager who maximizes their rewards and minimizes their punishment. When accurate information is not rewarded for its own sake, people tend to say instead what they think the boss wants to hear. Only when a crisis reaches the proportion where it can

no longer be concealed does the manager hear about the trouble and lament "Nobody is communicating around here."

3. The enemy of successful communication is the assumption that it has taken place perfectly. Every attempt to communicate results in only partial understanding. We cannot completely say what we mean or "tell it like it is" because each of us possesses different perceptions and perspectives. All we can hope for is a reasonable approximation in the transfer of meaning.

4. When communication breaks down, a natural response is to ask "Whose fault is it?" The effective manager, who is looking for results avoids this tendency and instead asks, "What can be done about it?"

Those administrators who recognize and apply these concepts will not only be better communicators but also more effective managers.

## REFERENCES

1. *The Houston Post*, October 16, 1977.
2. Carl Rogers, *On Becoming a Person*. Boston: Houghton Mifflin, 1961.
3. William H. Whyte, *Is Anybody Listening?* New York: Venture, 1952.
4. Active listening techniques are described in a variety of publications, including Thomas Gordon, *Parent Effectiveness Training*. Chicago: Wyden, 1971 and William C. Morris and Marshall Sashkin, *Organizational Behavior in Action*. St. Paul: West Publishing, 1976.
5. Cited in Mildred Newman and Bernard Berkowitz, *How to Be Your Own Best Friend*. New York: Random House, 1971.
6. Donald Scobel, "Doing Away with the Factory Blues," *Harvard Business Review*, November–December 1975, pp. 132–142.
7. See Gordon, *Parent Effectiveness*, and Morris and Sashkin, *Organizational Behavior*.

# CHAPTER 3
# HOW TO MEET
# WITH SUCCESS

Why have the meeting anyway? Why, especially, when managers and supervisors frequently complain that most of the meetings they attend are simply a waste of time? Meetings can be held without serving a useful purpose. They can be held for reasons that are more historical than practical—out of habit rather than by design. Having recognized that meetings are generally not highly regarded and that they may sometimes be merely an historical artifact, why are they convened so often? Why does almost every organization, be it corporate enterprise, government agency, church group, hospital board, or civic club, conduct most of its business at a meeting?

The reason is that, despite all of the things said against them, there is simply no better way to accomplish all of the things that even a poorly conducted meeting can achieve. Even though many matters in an organization could best be taken care of by someone who consults no one else or by a letter, a phone call, or a memo, a meeting still performs functions that will never be taken over by copying machines, telephones, tape recorders, computers, or closed-circuit TV monitors.

## WHY HOLD A MEETING?

Meetings, even when poorly planned and badly conducted, fulfill certain basic functions that no technological advance can replace. One of the most basic functions a meeting performs is to address the basic human need for affiliation or inclusion. The feeling of belonging is a powerful psychological need in most people and an important human motive. In fact, a person's affiliates can significantly affect that person's actions and feelings. This can especially be seen in the sports fans who so strongly identify with "their" team that either elation or despair fills their week, depending on the results of their favorite team's game.

The need for and effects of affiliation are basic to a person's self-concept, as well. Ask almost anyone the question "Who are you?" and the response will invariably include a description of the person's affiliations. Depending on the particular associations, responses will be such statements as "I'm a steelworker," "I'm a Catholic," "I'm a Mexican-American," or the like. The way we see ourselves is influenced by the groups to which we belong.

Perhaps that partially explains why Rensis Likert, a prominent management researcher at the University of Michigan, found that the most effective organizations he studied were characterized by a feeling of group pride. His studies indicated that a decisive factor in the performance of a particular organizational unit was the degree to which people met together, identified with one another, and sought to achieve organizational goals through collaborative efforts.[1]

Getting everyone together periodically cannot completely satisfy this human need for belonging, but it can go a long way toward providing for its fulfillment. Thus, one of the things that calling a meeting does is to define the unit, group, or team. Those who are invited belong to it, those who are not invited do not.

Another advantage is that when people consistently attend meetings to which they are invited, an enormous amount of things can be left unsaid that would otherwise have to be explained. This means that even ordinary meetings may be more efficient than is commonly supposed. For at a meeting, those present can update, clarify, or revise what is known and accepted by everyone in the unit. This shared pool of information and experiences not only helps each individual do a better job, but also improves the communication among them.

This capacity to share knowledge and experience among a number of people has been called "the social mind" of the group by meeting consultant Antony Jay. Jay describes it as the capacity of a group to act as one individual and to produce a result that is greater than the sum of the parts.[2] Even the ancient Greek poet Homer appreciated this peculiar source of power, which is latent in every meeting. He wrote at one point in *The Iliad,* "When many are got together, you can be guided by him whose counsel is wisest. . . . If a man is alone, he is less full of resource, and his wit is weaker." What Homer is saying is that, in a group, people can feel more comfortable about expressing their ideas and testing out a proposed option. If openness is encouraged, they are more likely to explore all options and to reach an agreement that everyone will accept because they know as individuals that they are backed by the group.

Making a group decision has the effect of giving people confidence in using a particular idea. Since the decision to apply the idea has been tested, shaped, and refined by the combined judgment and knowledge of several people, each individual tends to be more confident that it will work. Consequently, an original idea from one person not only is able to be objectively improved through discussion, but it is also empowered by the confidence that people tend to have in it after it has met the refining process of the meeting.

## WHAT A MEETING CAN DO

A meeting *can* perform all of the functions just described, but there is no guarantee that it *will* do so in every situation. Understanding the basic functions of a meeting, however, can be important for maximizing its value. Meetings are an important management tool when used appropriately and wisely. Unfortunately, many managers do not realize what a meeting can and cannot do and so either miss opportunities or waste time.

A distinct advantage of a meeting is that it tends to develop teamwork and cooperation among those who are required to coordinate their actions in order to be effective. A meeting can ensure that people in a group are pursuing the same goals, sharing pertinent information with one another, and meshing personal activities with common concerns.

Another advantage of a meeting is that it tends to make people action oriented. Holding a meeting can encourage people to take positions, make choices, and decide on alternatives. This can be an important advantage when a decision is needed on a particular course of action.

A third advantage of a meeting is that it tends to create in all present a common commitment. It is almost axiomatic in the research on management that involvement begets commitment. Conversely, not being consulted or included in a decision can result in resentment and opposition. Generally, people want to have some say over matters that affect them, and they are satisfied just knowing that their views are listened to and their ideas respected.

## WHAT A MEETING CANNOT DO

Meetings are not a panacea for organizational problems, they are simply one tool in the managerial tool kit. The importance and value of this tool should be neither overlooked nor overused. Meetings can serve a useful purpose *as long as they have a purpose.* The trouble is that too many meetings are convened without an explicit objective. Or, in the case of some meetings, the intended objectives of the agenda could be handled better by individual, not group, action. Agenda items of the typical meeting could be quite satisfactorily dealt with by a single person who consults no one.

Even though there are a host of advantages for holding a meeting, as previously highlighted, it should be recognized that many types of work are best accomplished outside the group setting. As a rule, for instance, individuals acting alone can more efficiently reach decisions on issues that are relatively simple in structure then can a group. Problems that have objectively separable elements or that require a strict series of sequential acts are also better suited for individual action.

Moreover, in meetings it is assumed not only that general facts are already shared by those attending, but also that they have some specific information on the matter at hand. Thus a meeting can promote the sharing of established facts but cannot generate new facts. Detailed, analytical work is difficult to do in a meeting as well, because participants do not have the flexibility of being able to consult various information sources.

A meeting can do many things if its specific limitations are recognized. Of course, just how effective a meeting is also depends on how it is conducted. To this end, there are important criteria, which are necessary ingredients for an effective meeting, to be met.

## CREATING A POSITIVE MEETING CLIMATE

A good meeting climate is essential for a productive meeting. Creating the proper atmosphere is as important for the progress of a meeting as it is for the growth of plants. It is necessary to give most plants proper amounts of water, fertilizer, and light, but good soil and proper attention cannot adequately compensate for a cold climate. Ideas, like plants, need time and the proper conditions, including the right climate, to develop. Here are some of the more important ways to develop a good meeting climate.

### Identify the group

It is important to describe meeting attendees as a group or team. Only when people at the meeting begin to identify with one another will they start to reap the benefits of participation. The meeting leader and group members can promote this identification by talking about "us," "our group," "what we want to accomplish," and "what action we intend to take."

## Share responsibility

The responsibility for an effective meeting is not limited to one person. A meeting in which only a few people take part and feel responsible for results is not a good meeting. Making individual assignments or requesting specific information from those who are not actively participating in the meeting can help them feel more responsible for the meeting's outcome.

## Maintain open communication

On almost every subject, proposal, or issue, people have both some ideas or opinions and some feelings or hunches. In order to completely explore a topic at a meeting, both types of data must be shared. Managers and supervisors tend not to share their feelings or hunches with others and, consequently, do not get others to share their intuitive ideas with them. Giving orders and making assignments is not sharing. Sharing is the process of getting everyone's thoughts and feelings out into the open before action is taken or a decision is made.

## Listen to understand

As previously discussed, a major barrier to interpersonal communication in meetings is the natural tendency of people to judge — to approve or disapprove — the statements made by other people. This can be illustrated quite simply. Suppose someone, commenting on an ongoing group discussion, says to you, "I didn't like what was just said." What would you say? Your reply would probably either approve or disapprove the perspective expressed. You would respond, "I didn't either," or something like, "Oh, I thought it was pretty good myself." The point is, each person tends to respond from an individual frame of reference. Moreover, the stronger the feelings expressed, the more likely that there will be no mutual element in the communication. There will be two ideas, two feelings, two judgments.

Is there any way to avoid this communication barrier? Yes, and it is simply this: To improve communication in a meeting, people must listen to understand before they evaluate. They must try to see an idea or a position from the other person's point of view or frame of reference. It may sound simple, but it is not very well known or used, and it can make a significant difference in the climate of a meeting.

### Develop trust

In order for people to openly express themselves at a meeting, they must feel confident that they have the respect of the others present. When people meet together for group discussion, they invariably wonder "Can I trust these people? Will they seek to understand my point of view? What should I tell them and what should I withhold?" Trust seems to operate according to the principle of reciprocity. That is, when people feel that they are accepted and trusted, they respond in kind by accepting and trusting. Such a relationship is seldom created all at once, but can be developed with time and consistency.

Trust is not something a person does. It is not a behavior that can be seen or observed. Rather, it is an evaluation or a conclusion reached after determining that another person is consistently honest and forthright. If people feel that a manager is open and honest with them, free from hidden agendas in a meeting, they will feel that the manager can be trusted and will actively participate in the meetings.

### PLANNING A MEETING

It is important to establish and maintain a good meeting climate in order to conduct successful meetings. Planning the meeting in advance is also important. Planning provides direction in the meeting for, as an old proverb says, "unless you know where you are going, any road will take you there."

In planning a meeting, the meeting leader should formulate answers to the following three questions:

1. What are my objectives? What results do I want this meeting to accomplish?

2.  As the manager, what kind of role is the most appropriate for me to adopt in this type of meeting?

3.  What questions or concerns might the others attending have about these topics?

## Set objectives

What a leader wants to accomplish, the objectives, is the first thing to decide in planning for a meeting. Meetings can only achieve certain types of objectives. Moreover, there should be a close match between the meeting format and the type of objective the meeting is supposed to reach. Meetings can be convened to exchange information, make a decision, uncover problems or opportunities, set goals, and initiate changes. Each type of meeting can achieve its purpose best if it is appropriately planned. For instance, if a meeting is called to exchange information, the leader should have previously determined that the information in question could not simply be distributed in document form. If certain facts must come from the leader, or if the information needs some clarification or comment, then it is wise to have it explained in a meeting.

Sometimes a meeting is called to solve a specific problem or make a decision on some matter. For instance, a meeting might be called to get ideas from employees on how to improve productivity. When all the people get together to engage in such actions, it is more likely that all appropriate facts will surface. Since a variety of perspectives will probably be shared, there is also an increased likelihood for a good solution. Two heads, as any good meeting leader will tell you, are indeed better than one.

Robert Townsend, former president of Avis Rent-A-Car, goes one step further than that adage. He maintains that two problem-solving meetings are better than one. Townsend contends that at the first meeting alternatives can be generated and priorities established. But if the leader will wait a day before making a decision, the convictions of those who decide quickly and the commitment of those who decide more slowly will both be secured. This method, Townsend says, makes problem-solving meetings more thoughtful and therefore more productive.

A third type of meeting that can be called is for uncovering problems or opportunities. This is similar to doing preventive maintenance work on a piece of machinery. Just as good lubrication and periodic tune-ups keep equipment in good working order, occasional group sessions check on how things are going in order to keep problems from developing. When a work group takes the time to occasionally critique their means of accomplishing tasks, they are likely to see ways to improve their methods. Such meetings can help people see both "the forest *and* the trees."

A fourth type of meeting gets everyone involved in planning future activities and setting short-term goals. Goal setting gives people a target to aim at and lets them know how well they are doing. For example, setting productivity or safety goals through group involvement increases the likelihood that the goals will be achieved.

Finally, a meeting can develop teamwork by helping a manager implement a policy change. Changing the way things are done can be disturbing to people if such changes threaten either their status or their security. At whatever level in an organization changes are decided on, they must have the support of those who are affected by them if they are to be effective. Meeting to decide how to implement such things as an Equal Employment Opportunity (EEO) policy or a benefits change decided on at upper levels can secure the group's commitment to abide by the particular guideline.

### Select a role

These are the five types of meetings a manager might call, depending on the particular objectives in mind. After the objectives have been stated, the meeting leader can then select an appropriate role. Basically, the variations available to a manager range from controlling and directing to monitoring and standard setting.

If a manager is giving out information or instructing workers on a particular technique, then a direct and straightforward style should be used. This is a typical role for an information exchange meeting. On the other hand, if the purpose of a meeting is to explore options, find alternatives, or start something new, a manager should act more like an umpire than a radio announcer. Creative sessions require a manager to listen to every point of view and encourage others to speak out. Such meetings require two-way communication because they are convened to achieve two-way actions. In any meeting that is more than an information exchange a supervisor should do all that is possible to get others to express themselves and contribute their own ideas.

### Anticipate questions

The third factor a manager must consider in preparing a meeting has to do with the questions or concerns that participants might have about the topic. One way to formulate this factor is to make a mental checklist of what newspaper reporters call "the five W's and the H." By asking *who, what, when, where, why,* and *how*, a leader can better anticipate any questions or concerns that others at the meeting might have and thereby prepare appropriate responses to them. Good meetings, like many other things, do not just happen; someone must make them happen. Preparing for a meeting by creating a written meeting guide can also help.

### HOW TO MANAGE A MEETING

Once a leader has prepared a meeting guide, the meeting is definitely headed in the right direction. But that is not all there is to it. Just as the driver of a car has two tasks, to follow the route and to manage the vehicle, a manager's job can be divided into two corresponding tasks once the planning is complete. These tasks are to deal with the subject and to deal with the people.

### Handling the topic

At the start of any meeting the leader should indicate what results the session should accomplish. This means explicitly describing previously formulated objectives. Like any other work standards, this statement of objectives allows the group to monitor its progress and to evaluate its performance when the work appears to be complete. In addition, the leader's job in conducting a meeting is to summarize key subject points. Writing them on a chart pad or blackboard can help in such a summary. This ensures a common understanding of what has been discussed. A final role of the leader in dealing with the subject of a meeting is to end a discussion when it becomes clear that (a) more facts are required before further progress can be made, (b) the meeting needs the views of people who are not present, or (c) there is apparent agreement on the topic.

## Handling the people

The other part of a manager's role in a meeting is to deal with the people, practicing communication techniques that maintain control of the group. Basically, this involves asking appropriate questions at the proper time, which keeps everyone involved and interested in the topic. A leader manages the discussion through the judicious use of *effective* questions. The following table illustrates the type and purpose of various questions. Learning how and when to ask the right questions in a meeting is an important managerial task. It is the core of a leader's control in dealing with the people at a meeting.

Asking questions at the right time helps keep a meeting moving and the participants tuned in. There is probably nothing so destructive to a meeting as a discussion that is rambling or otherwise out of control. Here are some tips that good leaders practice to help manage the people and maintain control.

1. *Stimulate the discussion.* A meeting leader might have to begin a discussion by asking several open questions and then asking more direct questions as a follow-up.

2. *Balance the discussion.* It seems that nothing "turns off" an entire group as much as one person whose mouth is locked in the "on" position. Interrupt when necessary, and make sure everyone is included in the discussion.

3. *Avoid polarization.* Sometimes disagreement flares into active conflict. The two opposing parties themselves may

### Question Techniques for Meeting Leading

| Type of Question | Purpose | Example |
|---|---|---|
| Open | To generate ideas | "How do you see this situation?" |
| Direct | To probe | "What is your experience with this situation?" |
| Piggyback | To include others<br>To gain commitment from others | "How do you feel about what was just said?" |
| Reflective | To remain neutral<br>To check others' views | "That sounds reasonable. How would you proceed?" |
| Analytical | To evaluate | "What are the advantages and disadvantages of such an approach?" |

feel uncomfortable about the situation but may not know how to get out of it without losing face. At such times the meeting leader can restore order by asking piggyback questions, bringing others into the discussion and easing tensions.

4. *Keep the meeting lively.* A leader enlivens a meeting by changing pace—telling an anecdote, using a chart pad, or moving on to another topic. It is important that a manager be aware of the nonverbal messages from others at the meeting in order to perform this function sufficiently.

5. *Reach a conclusion.* A meeting is not finished unless everyone attending can plainly state what the session accomplished and what action is to be taken next.

## MAKING IT A GOOD MEETING

At the end of the discussion of each agenda item, the meeting leader should briefly summarize what has been said. This helps the participants to see that something has been accomplished or produced in the meeting. Then assignments should be made and deadlines attached to every action. Everyone should be clear about what has transpired and who will do what. This is very important. A postmeeting evaluation of how the group worked together is another valuable tool that many managers have found to be useful.

Meetings are not a panacea for managerial ills; however, nor are they a contributor to them unless they are poorly conducted. Meetings provide a time and place to make decisions, a purpose that cannot be ignored, and some product results from every effective meeting. Any manager can meet with success if the guidelines described in this chapter are adhered to.

## REFERENCES

1.  Rensis Likert, *New Patterns of Management*. New York: McGraw-Hill, 1961.
2.  Antony Jay, "How to Run a Meeting," *Harvard Business Review*, March–April 1976, pp. 43–57.

# CHAPTER 4
# IMPLEMENTING
# ORGANIZATIONAL
# DEVELOPMENT

Organizational development (OD) means different things to different people. To some, OD is any effort that consciously attempts to improve organizational performance. To others, OD involves very specific procedures that focus on improving interpersonal relations in an organizational unit. To still others, it involves a systems analysis of such things as the relationship between the organization and its environment, the tasks to be done and the individuals to do them, the formal policy of the organization, and the unwritten codes of conduct that people follow.[1]

The following is a limited, more focused view of OD. It is not intended to represent the entire field of knowledge that has come to be called by that name. What it does attempt to do is provide an introduction to managers, describing some ways in which they can use OD to improve the functioning of their particular work units. The emphasis is on problem finding rather than on problem solving or decision making, an emphasis that is too often neglected by managers and supervisors.

## AN OVERVIEW OF OD

OD is not another motivational program. It is not training. It is not even a set of identifiable activities. It is instead a means of recognizing the ways in which an organization operates, of understanding what makes the organization the way it is, of being very explicit about how it should be, and of developing methods to make it that way. It emphasizes that *how* things are done in a work setting are at least as important as *what* things are done.

Every organization possesses two conditions. One has to do with organizational output or consequences and the other with organizational dynamics or methods. Most of the time the performance of organizational units is measured strictly in terms of output: production, costs, turnover, absenteeism, and the like. But these outputs are affected by various organizational dynamics that, although measured less frequently, are also important. Commitment, involvement, and satisfaction are just some of the possible ways to measure organizational dynamics.[2]

The distinction between organizational output and dynamics can be highlighted by comparing an organizational unit to a complex piece of machinery. The piece of machinery is designed to produce some output, such as loaves of bread, aluminum cans, or cardboard boxes. But to achieve that output it must be lubricated, have worn parts replaced, and have all gears mesh. This is directly analogous to organizational functioning. In order for people in an organization to achieve output objectives they must share the organization's goals, priorities, and procedures.

One way to get employee commitment, researchers have consistently found, is by getting employees involved in matters that affect their organizational lives. The essence of the involvement principle is that employees are most productive and satisfied when they are included in the establishment of some of their own goals and procedures.[3]

## OBJECTIVES OF OD

Getting employees involved in various organizational matters is a basic aspect of OD, but the involvement must be appropriate and directed. How to go about getting workers involved will be discussed in a later section on strategies in OD. What to do to maximize their involvement will be discussed in the section on characteristics of OD. Why get them involved at all will be discussed next.

OD attempts to supplement the usual downward flow of information with some communication moving upward. It attempts to do this by getting all of those who work in an organizational unit involved in the assessment of how well things are going. Managers, with all of the demands inherent in their position, cannot know enough or control enough to run the whole show.

OD can achieve five primary objectives when conscientiously applied at the supervisory level. These are:

1. to increase employee identification with the organization;
2. to increase employee identification with the work group;
3. to increase employee commitment;
4. to expand the perspective of all workers;
5. to assist the manager in actively managing the work.

### Identification with the organization

Appropriate employee involvement can increase employee identification with the organization as a whole, because employees realize that their views count, their input matters, and their concerns will be heard. When managers get employees involved by asking for feedback on how things are going in the total work situation, they are implicitly communicating that the employees' ideas are valued. People tend to mirror the way they are supervised and will therefore often respond to such supervisory concern by increasing their concern for the work they are doing. By asking for information a supervisor is also implicitly saying "I will listen to you and will respond to your ideas and concerns, and no third party is necessary." A sensitive manager with OD skills is an effective link between labor and management.

The importance of the supervisors's communicating this concern and the need for an increase in employee identification with the organizations they work for has taken on a new urgency. The apparent antagonism of the public at large toward most institutions is matched in some organizations by internal dissent and discontent. The need for a different arrangement between supervisor and supervised can be seen in many places. One article in the management literature noted that there is widespread feeling against management, from managers as well as from employees. For example, business advisors Dan Fenn and Daniel Yankelovich maintain that the following statements are representative of the feelings of many people in a variety of organizations:

- "Management here doesn't care about people; the people up the line are inadequate and insensitive."
- "Management is still trying to run this company the way it did twenty years ago."
- "I'm a good company man, I've been a good company man all my life; but damn it, there are some times when you should just stand up and protest."
- "We're very suspicious here of anything that management does; we're always looking for booby traps."[4]

Attitudes like these are often the basis for establishing unions to counterbalance managerial authority. They can also be revealed in reduced effort and increased scrap rates or in overt actions against minority policies and programs. All of these actions are founded in the belief that managers exercise their authority in an arbitrary manner. Perhaps only through asking for feedback and getting employees involved can a manager offset this belief.

## Identification with the work group

A second objective of OD is to increase the identification of employees with their work group. Everyone needs to identify with a reference group and derive support from it. By periodically getting all members of a work group together to assess how things are going, this objective can be realized.

A number of influential writers have described work in modern society as basically dehumanizing.[5] They say that people do not have adequate opportunities for dignity and fulfillment. The root issue in the dialogue that has emerged between these writers and managers who defend current practices seems to be that there are too few opportunities for status or influence for those who are not high flyers. "Getting ahead," the traditional criterion of success, can simply not be everyone's lot. When it is the only opportunity that organizations provide, many must necessarily feel dissatisfied. OD can expand opportunities for status and influence through employee involvement and the utilization of an expanded set of values.

## Commitment

A third objective of OD is to increase employee commitment. It is an accepted truism that involvement is a precondition for commitment. When people have a chance to influence things that are going on around them they are much more likely to put forth effort. They feel trusted and important, and these personal feelings are real keys to individual productive functioning.[6]

One management researcher has found that, whenever people in an organization are asked what they would wish the organization to be like, they have consistently preferred to participate more in various decisions that affect them.[7] They do not necessarily want to make the decision, but they do want their input to influence it. When they feel that their input is influential, the employees tend to be more productive and more satisfied than their "unheard from" counterparts.

## Expanded perspective

A fourth objective of OD is to expand everyone's perspective. Through mutual interaction and exchange, employees can find out more about how their own particular work affects the total organization's goals. Instead of seeing their own limited area, employees are exposed to the way other people see things. In this way, OD actively promotes lateral communication.

This is very important for an increasing number of large organizations. As Robert Tannebaum and Shel Davis have indicated:

> Many organizations today, particularly those at the leading edge of technology, are faced with ferment and flux. In increasing instances, the bureaucratic model—with its emphasis on relatively rigid structure, well-defined functional specialization, direction and control exercised through a formal hierarchy of authority, fixed system of rights, duties and procedures, and relative impersonality of human relationships—is responding inadequately to demands placed upon it from the outside and from within the organization.[8]

## Assist management

The fifth objective of OD is to assist the manager in actively managing the unit. It is easy for a manager to get caught up in shuffling paper and responding to routine demands. It requires effort to be proactive and to discover issues before they become crises. The tendency for the routine to take precedence over the creative is simply a result of too much to do and too little time to do it.

Although no one can be given more time than there is, OD strategies can give managers better control over the time they do have. It achieves this in two ways: (1) it gives a manager better information on how employees are feeling about things, and (2) it develops more committed and responsible employees, thereby reducing the time and concern a manager might spend in follow-up activities.

Each of these five objectives is possible and achievable through planned OD. As previously mentioned, OD is a managerial posture that has certain characteristics as well as a general set of strategies. It can improve organizational output by improving organizational dynamics when consistently applied. Managers looking downward may have some reservations about

OD as it has been presented. It does, after all, call for at least some sharing of managerial authority. But just as it informally shares authority, so it also informally shares responsibility because people feel more responsible.

Perhaps the greatest significance of OD as described is that it creates a sense of balance in supervision. It provides employees with a method for identifying what they think is important and for doing something about it, while at the same time they assist managers in identifying and capitalizing on available opportunities to improve the work. It is quite likely that each of the five objectives described will be realized if OD is applied in the manner presented in the following sections.

## OD CHARACTERISTICS

The burden of creating an open, problem-solving climate in an organizational unit rests squarely with the manager of that work group. If a manager tends to manage in ways that decrease others' self-esteem and integrity, they will tend to behave in ways that confirm the manager's negative notions of them. The inverse is also true. The fact that this "self-fulfilling prophecy" exists means that accurately communicating positive expectations to employees can actually increase their productivity.[9] It is up to the manager to find ways to communicate positive expectations to workers. It is a manager's responsibility to find a vehicle, or if you will, an excuse for meeting collectively with employees to discuss ways in which the unit goes about its work.

Just as individuals develop habits, work groups develop habits. Some of these habits are so basic to the things that either individuals or work groups do that neither are very aware of how these habits shape and condition behavior. Habits are not in and of themselves either good or bad. In work groups, they can be either advantageous or disadvantageous, depending on whether they help or hinder the work and workers.

Sometimes the unwritten rules about "the ways things are done around here" get in a work unit's way. One way to find out about a work unit's habits and to determine how people feel about them is to spend some time critiquing performance. By taking the time to sit back and reflect on various unwritten policies, people in a work unit can understand each other better and work together more cooperatively. This is what OD is all about.

## STRATEGIES FOR APPLYING OD

OD strategies are those activities a manager plans in order to find out ways to improve either job productivity or job satisfaction. The activities that will be described in this section are designed to improve an organizational unit's functioning by getting employees involved in assessing its current state and planning for a future condition. Three kinds of strategies are going to be described, each with its own purpose. The first strategy deals with improving work practices and is called an *information gathering session*. The second strategy deals with group practices and is called a *procedure analyzing session*. The third strategy deals with supervisory practices and is called an *impact examining session*. How to conduct each of these sessions is described. Remember, the overall purpose of each strategy is planned unit maintenance and appropriate unit change.

### Information gathering session

An information gathering session may be convened to address a specific problem, handle a particular opportunity, or simply check in on how things are going. The content of such a session could focus on such specifics as schedules, equipment, or supplies. But the content could also be more general, dealing with goals, objectives, or priorities. The content may even be just a year-end evaluation of all operations. The key to a good session is a willingness on everyone's part to openly participate. Some general ways to encourage such participation have already been presented. Specifically, here's how a manager conducts an information gathering session.

Begin by calling a meeting of all of those in the work unit who can be scheduled for at least one hour. Announce that the meeting's purpose is to look at current work practices. (If there is a more specific purpose, describe it.) This lets everyone know exactly what the manager's intentions are and reduces any initial suspicion about what is wanted or expected.

Indicate at the start of the session that to get the necessary information it would be best to keep all responses anonymous. To do this, distribute three $4 \times 6$ file cards to each person and ask everyone to write "helps" on one, "blocks" on the second, and "suggestions" on the third. Everyone should answer each of the following questions and record the answers on the appropriate card.

1. What do you like about this work unit that you want to maintain? (helps)
2. What keeps either you or this work unit from functioning as effectively as possible? (blocks)
3. If we were operating together perfectly, how would things be done differently? (suggestions)

The first two questions ask workers to decide what is already useful and what could be improved in the work environment. The third question asks them to decide what they think should be done about either. Indicate that, once everyone has finished responding to these questions, the cards will be passed to a fellow employee (select and announce the name), who will record the results. All cards will then be destroyed to protect anonymity.

When everyone has had a chance to respond to these questions, the cards should then be passed to the recorder. The recorder should make three piles, one each of helps, blocks, and suggestions. As the contents of each pile are read aloud, another employee should write the items mentioned on three separate sheets of chart paper or in three separate columns on a blackboard. A tick mark should be placed beside an item whenever it is repeated instead of recording it again as another entry.

There is now a list of issues, arranged by priority, that affect those present. This list can then constitute the agenda for the remainder of the session. Spend a few minutes highlighting the items mentioned in the "helps" column, and then break the employees into groups of four or five people to clarify those items mentioned under "blocks." Finally, in the same small groups, employees should "brainstorm" (i.e., have a free-wheeling discussion without evaluating ideas), using items in the "suggestions" column to help them get started.

Managers should have a clear idea about how people feel about their work and working conditions following such a session. The information obtained could then be used later to help decide where to focus managerial attention. These decisions may be made alone or with the aid of workers, but the decision making should follow and not be a part of the information gathering session. Of course, it is critical that managers find a way, either through a follow-up meeting, memo, or bulletin board notice, to inform every employee on the outcome of each idea, proposal, or suggestion.

### Procedure analyzing session

The purpose of a procedure analyzing session is to get employees to carefully examine the things they do as a group. This includes such unwritten codes of conduct as relationships between people, communication procedures, conflict resolution methods, and so forth. The value of having such a session is analogous to having a medical checkup. A checkup helps a person plan for the future as well as discover how things are going in the present. People and organizational units who do not have checkups find out something is wrong only when a crisis finally develops. Then it is often too late.

A procedure analyzing session is one way to get employees involved in assessing standards and consciously structuring new group practices. It is a way of looking at the way people work together in order to improve the productive functioning of all. Groups and group behavior, with their unwritten codes of conduct, are a fact of organizational life. Like all other organizational practices, they need to be consciously managed.

Prior to the actual session, employees should individually write down examples of behavior that lead to either productive or nonproductive functioning in the work group. A good way to do this is through the use of a questionnaire. (See Appendix I p. 101 for a sample questionnaire.) These individual reactions can then be combined and listed according to importance, with suggestions for improvement included, as in an information gathering session.

Sometimes in conducting a procedure analyzing session, there is a tendency to focus on why people do things in certain ways (e.g., ignoring people's suggestions). This should be avoided. Focusing on why tends to reduce the effectiveness of the session because it increases feelings of defensiveness. People feel accused and therefore try to defend their behavior.

A more productive approach is to focus on the how of behavior. The group members should describe *what* they see people doing and *how* they see these actions affecting the group's functioning. The target is then on change and improvement. That means the two most important questions to answer in a procedure analyzing session are:

1. What group practices do we have that enhance or hinder our effectiveness?
2. How can we do things differently in order to be more effective?

Here are some step-by-step guides for planning and conducting a procedure analyzing session.

1. Begin by determining the willingness of group members to assess how they work together. If they are willing, distribute a questionnaire (see p. 101 for an example) several days before the scheduled session.
2. Have workers give their completed questionnaires to a pre-selected peer so that the main points can be summarized before the session. After these points are recorded as agenda items, the completed questionnaires should be destroyed.
3. The actual session should then deal not with who said what but with the following question applied to each agenda item: "What must we do to either change an undesirable condition or maintain a desirable one?"

4. The role of the members is to provide data and discuss possible action plans. Your role is to understand their positions and acknowledge their input. No decision should be made at this time to either accept or reject any of the suggestions.

5. At a subsequent session, with the assistance of group members, complete the problem-solving cycle by (a) analyzing the information to see if the issues are symptoms or root concerns, and (b) evaluating the appropriateness of each suggestion.

## Impact examining session

It is difficult for anyone to do all of the right things at the right time. For that reason, it is important to get feedback on how the things we do affect others. It is especially important for a manager because that person **is** required to routinely influence others and direct them in the achievement of organizational output. Getting feedback on the manager's impact on others also helps achieve those ends.

Feedback on personal managerial practices is important information that is not easily shared by people in lower status positions in the organization. In fact, the risks are so great that most employees simply remain silent. A manager is more likely to receive sensitive feedback when workers feel safe or even rewarded for sharing such information. They are more likely to give it when they are convinced that there will be no repercussions.

To ensure anonymity, divide the unit members into small groups of four or five people at a planned impact examining session. These subgroups would meet for 30 to 40 minutes following the introduction, which might be phrased something like this:

> I am concerned about the impact which my managerial practices are having on you individually and collectively. I would appreciate it if you could help me improve them. I would like to have each of you identify those things which I do or fail to do which seems to reduce the effectiveness of our particular unit. I would also like to have you tell

me those things which you think I do well and which you would like to see me continue doing.

I will not be present while you meet and you can just turn in a written summary to me later today or tomorrow. No names need be mentioned or included. I'm not interested in knowing who said what, but I am interested in improvement and valid information.[10]

Just as technical equipment requires an occasional tune-up and some preventive maintenance work from time to time, so too does the human machinery in an organizational unit. Each of the OD strategies that have been described can perform this function in various ways and thereby help a work unit maintain peak performance and efficiency.

## SUMMARY

Being a manager is not an easy task. For good reasons, the manager has often been described as being "in the middle." A multitude of relationships must be carefully managed if the unit is to be effectively controlled. In today's organizations, "Who's in control?" is a much more valid question than "Who's in charge?" Control, which is a function of information, is a more useful concept for describing the responsibility of a supervisor than the traditional concept of authority.

The classic way of describing a manager's role has been to say that it includes authority over certain people and things that is equal to the amount of responsibility assumed. This view maintains that it is improper to make a manager responsible for certain functions without also giving the authority to make decisions concerning those functions. However, there may be many instances in the modern organization where responsibility does exceed authority. A manager's responsibility for upholding EEO standards without having authority in such matters is just one example.

Recognizing that "who's in control" is more important than "who's in charge" leads to realizing the importance of developing and maintaining effective lines of communication. The strategy sessions that have been described can help managers do just that. They foster two-way communication on an ongoing basis. Of course, to be effective, they cannot be used as a manipulative technique but must be used to express the values and characteristics that have also been described. Implementing such OD sessions on a regular basis is good for employees because they have a chance to influence their workday world. It is also good for managers because they can more effectively supervise their business using the particular kinds of information that surfaces in each type of strategy session. Such sessions put managers in control, as long as they focus the units' attention on the problems that members can help to solve.

Some managers may find it difficult to adapt to this style of managing. They may feel that by involving employees they will have less instead of more control. This is a valid and natural concern that must be addressed in order for any of the three sessions just described to be successful. This can be done by doing the following three things:

1. by allowing a group of managers to meet together to learn about the rationale behind OD;
2. by giving them an opportunity to let their concerns surface in subgroups and then discuss these concerns;
3. by providing them with process consultants as resources, if desired.

Some employees may initially question the motives of a manager who convenes an OD session. They may wonder if this is simply a management gimmick to get higher productivity without giving workers a pay increase. If this is a concern, the manager who is confronted with such feelings might say something like this:

> The real experts at identifying and solving problems in this work group are all of you. You know better than anyone else what it's like to work here. You know what things need to be done to make this both a high producing unit and a good place to work. By maintaining productivity at a high level, job security is ensured for all of us. Perhaps

you may have asked yourself, when you saw a bad situation, "Why don't they straighten this out? Don't they know it's costing the company money?" Well, what we are trying to do is to get your ideas and input about what goes on here so that the "they" becomes "we." What I want to do is to have all of us feel that we can affect what goes on around here.

It takes time and effort to do all of the things that have been presented, but they are well worth it. A manager who consistently utilizes the OD skills that have been detailed can expect to realize the five objectives mentioned in a previous section. However, as with other good managerial practices, they won't work unless they are applied.

## REFERENCES

1. Thoman H. Patten, Jr., Terry F. Skjervheim, and Jack L. Shook, *Characteristics and Professional Concerns of Organization Development Practitioners.* Madison, Wis.: ASTD, OD Division, 1973.

2. William G. Dyer, *Insight to Impact.* Provo, Ut.: Brigham Young University Press, 1976.

3. See, for example, William J. Roche and Neil L. Mackinnon, "Motivating People with Meaningful Work," *Harvard Business Review,* May–June 1970, pp. 97–110.

4. Dan H. Fenn and Daniel Yankelovich, "Responding to the Employee Voice," *Harvard Business Review,* May–June 1972, pp. 83–91.

5. Roger Ricklefs, "The Quality of Work," *Exploring the New Management,* ed. Robert M. Fulmer and Theodore T. Herbert. New York: Macmillian, 1974, pp. 211–215.

6. Norman C. Hill, "Self-Esteem: The Key to Effective Leadership," *Administrative Management,* August 1976, pp. 24–25, 50.

7. Rensis Likert, *The Human Organization.* New York: McGraw-Hill, 1967.

8. Robert Tannenbaum, and Sheldon A. Davis, "Values, Man, and Organizations," *Industrial Management Review,* Vol. X, 1969, pp. 67–86.

9. Robert Rosenthal, "The Pygmalion Effect Lives," *Psychology Today,* July 1973, pp. 56–59.

10. Dyer, *Insight to Impact.*

# PART II
# THE INTERPERSONAL
# FUNCTION

# CHAPTER 5
# SELF-ESTEEM
# AND THE SELF-FULFILLING
# PROPHECY

In everything we do or fail to do, we communicate attitudes and values that others take as cues to their own behavior. To what extent the positions we project are picked up by others, however, depends largely on the confidence people sense that we have in ourselves and in our points of view. Our communicated attitudes and expectations act as self-fulfilling prophecies when we really believe in them ourselves.

This notion of a self-fulfilling prophecy based on attitudes and expectations has long been recognized by behavioral scientists, therapists, and doctors. The existing evidence for the effects of these interpersonal self-fulfilling prophecies is almost overwhelming. Yet, their findings have not been widely communicated nor their implications for action generally understood.

## EXPECTATION AND PERFORMANCE

The findings of these researchers have some clear implications for managers. The research suggests that what a confident manager expects of those supervised significantly affects their performance. If a manager's actions communicate high but realistic performance expectations, it has the effect on employees of setting up a target they want to reach. But if the actions communicate low expectations, no such incentive will be created.

These findings on management through confident action and the creation of positive expectations that others want to fulfill point to a management style that is needed today. In recent years, the dilemma of trying to find an appropriate management style has put many managers between the "rock" of overpermissiveness and the "hard place" of unacceptable authoritarianism. Placed in this quandary between yielding too much and too little, many managers have vacillated between the two, and others have seen them as wishy-washy.

A new balance is needed between supervisor and supervised. Most people want certainty in their lives and are willing to go to great lengths to make those who are close to them predictable. This natural tendency partially explains why the self-fulfilling prophecy works. We do not like to be surprised. An ordinary example illustrates this. When led to expect that you are about to meet a pleasant person, your treatment at the first meeting may, in fact, make that person more pleasant. But if led to expect that you shall meet an unpleasant person, you may be so defensive that you force that person into unpleasant behavior toward you.

A high school principal put this idea to a test one year to see if it really worked. Throughout the school year, when substitute teachers were needed in various classrooms, he would distribute biographies of the substitute prior to his or her arrival. The biographies were identical except that half described the substitute as a "warm, concerned, supportive" person, and half described the substitute as a "cold, rigid, demanding person." Substantial differences resulted, both in the students' subsequent evaluation of the teacher and in their interaction patterns.

The students who expected the substitute to be warm and supportive rated him or her higher as an effective teacher and interacted frequently. Those who were led to believe that the substitute was cold and rigid had less to do with this teacher and rated him or her poorly.[1]

Whether a person believes others think that individual is important powerfully affects the person. This certainly includes family and friends as well as co-workers and supervisors. Since supervisors and managers have the authority to alter a person's status at the workplace, they can dramatically affect that person's self-image. Rare is the person who can be productive and feel proud when treated poorly by supervisors and others at work.

## THE PYGMALION EFFECT

This was the point George Bernard Shaw was trying to make in the play "Pygmalion," the basis for the musical hit "My Fair Lady." In the play, Shaw describes how Professor Higgins, an expert in languages and dialects, takes a London flower girl out of poverty and, within a matter of months, is able to pass her off at a celebrity ball as a princess. Near the conclusion of the story, the girl, Eliza Doolittle, explains to Higgins' mother the reason for her development. It was not the result of the professor's teaching ability, but of Mrs. Higgins' belief in Eliza. Eliza explained it this way:

> You see, really and truly, apart from the things anyone can pick up—the dressing and the proper way of speaking, and so on—the difference between a lady and a flower girl is not how she behaves, but how she's treated. I shall always be a flower girl to Professor Higgins, because he always treats me as a flower girl, and always will; but I know I can be a lady to you, because you always treat me as a lady and always will.

This operation of a self-fulfilling prophecy (or the Pygmalion effect, as it is sometimes called), based on expectations and the subsequent treatment of others works in both directions. That is, people tend to fulfill the expectations of others whether they are positive or not. Every organization and every manager provide employees with a sense of what is expected of them. If the expectations are sparse or lax, then people will exert little effort. If the expectations are negative, then people will be submissive, but act out what they think is really expected of them. However, if much is expected of employees in an organization, then chances are people will expect much of themselves. It is possible to create an atmosphere that encourages effort and vigorous performance. It is possible to establish a climate where people want to fulfill the expectations of those who guide and direct them.

The importance of creating high performance expectations has been suggested as a critical factor, distinguishing highly productive organizational units from less productive units, by Rensis Likert, founder of the Institute for Social Research at the University of Michigan. After two decades of research, Likert concluded that managers could use any number of motivational programs and still get either no return or a negative return for their time and money investment. What *did* make a difference in motivation and productivity, Likert discovered, was the manager's expectations of employee performance.[2]

### "Sweeney's miracle"

The concept of expectations influencing performance is also dramatically illustrated in the case of "Sweeney's miracle." James Sweeney taught industrial management and psychiatry at Tulane University in the mid-1960s. He was also responsible for the operation and administration of the university's Biomedical Computer Center. In his capacity as administrator, Sweeney directed a staff of people ranging from data programmers to maintenance workers. It was Sweeney's expectation that he could make a poorly educated black janitor into a competent computer operator. So he convinced George Johnson, a janitor at the computer center, to spend his free afternoons learning about computers.

Johnson was learning a great deal when a university administration official approached Sweeney and indicated that all operators were required to pass an IQ test before being allowed into the center. Johnson took the test and flunked. His test results indicated that he did not have the capacity to learn to type, much less to program a computer. Still, Sweeney was convinced of his own ability to teach Johnson to run a computer. He convinced the university administration to let Johnson stay on, promising them some positive results from his efforts. Within months, Johnson was so proficient at programming that he was asked to train new employees in the operation of the center.[3]

Sweeney's miracle was not the first time that the self-fulfilling prophecy was observed in the world of work. In 1890 a new type of tabulating machine known as the Hollerith was installed in various locations of the United States Census Bureau. The new equipment, similar to a typewriter, required the clerks' learning a new skill. The inventor of the machine, Hollerith, regarded the skill as quite demanding and expected that a trained worker could punch only about 550 cards a day. After a couple of weeks, when the workers had completed training, they began to produce at the expected rate of 550 cards per day. During the next few months some of the workers began to exceed the expected performance amount, but became so tense and upset that they were discouraged from doing this by the Secretary of the Interior.

Then a new group of about 200 clerks was employed. These people knew nothing about the Hollerith machine and had no knowledge of the previous standards. They were trained and assigned to locations separate from the previous group of employees. No expected performance standard was communicated, except that the employees were encouraged to do all that they could. Within three days this new group was producing at the top level reached by their predecessors. Whereas the earlier group was exhausted if they turned out 700 cards per day, the new group did two or three times that number with no apparent side effects. They did not have a limiting expectation and so were able to do more than the initial group of workers.

## UNCONSCIOUS ATTITUDE AND PERFORMANCE

Although it is important for managers to establish and communicate high performance expectations in order to reap their benefits, it is not an easy task to do. In fact, the things we *consciously* do will have no impact if they are not congruent with the things we *unconsciously* do. The actions we are hardly aware of often communicate what we expect of others. Somehow, regardless of the things we may overtly do or say, what we really believe comes through.

In other words, our attitude shows. Our attitude is reflected in the way we do things and profoundly affects the impact we have on others. A prominent management writer, Douglas MacGregor, maintains that our attitude, or what he calls the assumptions we make about human nature, is the determinant of a manager's influence on others. MacGregor asserts that, as long as managers feel that their employees are lazy, don't want to work, and lack ambition, even if they tell the workers otherwise, they will not be believed.[4] For instance, if a manager delegates a project to an employee with the words "I really trust you and know you can handle it," but then requires the employee to get authorization before making any decision regarding the project, the employee will realize that the manager's words are hollow.

Managers' unconscious negative or low expectations of employee performance always shine through, because the actions that communicate most are often those that are least obvious. Positive expectations, on the other hand, are difficult for managers to communicate and to use as part of their managerial style, because they require the mastery of some specific skills in order to be accurately conveyed. While these skills can be learned, their effective use depends on two crucial factors. These are (1) managers' confidence in themselves and in their own abilities, and (2) managers' belief in the ability of those being supervised.

These two factors indicate that a positive self-fulfilling prophecy is not available to the cynical manipulator. This is because our projections actually reflect our beliefs about ourselves and others, and they must complement what we do in order for desirable results to be obtained. What managers do must be consistent with what they believe in order to produce a positive result.

This was demonstrated several years ago when a group of managers attended a leadership training course. The seminar was geared toward acquainting them with the research evidence on interpersonal self-fulfilling prophecies and toward having them practice skills for communicating positive expectations to others. A review of the evidence was included, in order to convince the managers of the utility of the skills that were to be taught.

Several of those who attended saw this idea as merely a gimmick, which they could apply to get better performance from those they supervised without making any personal changes. Not only did these managers not experience the increased results they had hoped for, but some even experienced negative results. Employees in their units became resentful of the unrealistic quotas that were imposed on them and of the insincerity of their bosses. Turnover and absenteeism increased while productivity declined.

## Horse sense

What we *believe* counts as much as what we *do* when it comes to self-fulfilling prophecies. The things that we often don't realize we do generally come through loud and clear. This is amply illustrated by an incident that occurred around the turn of this century in Germany. It is about a horse known as Clever Hans.

Van Osten, the owner of Clever Hans, was a school teacher who was curious about the possibility of teaching animals how to answer arithmetic problems. He began to teach his horse every evening to tap out, with one of his hooves, answers to problems that would be presented to him. Hans became so good at clopping out just the right number of strokes that his owner began to exhibit him at local fairs. For any problem that was given to him, including alegbraic equations, Hans invariably tapped out the correct solution. In fact, he could even get right answers that required him to read and spell.

Hans' ability became so well known that a state appointed commission was organized to investigate Van Osten and the purported ability of his horse to think rationally and compute numbers correctly. In order to determine whether Van Osten was giving Hans some kind of sign to begin and stop tapping, the commission prohibited Han's owner from being present during the investigation. One by one the commissioners would whisper a complex arithmetic problem into Hans' ear, and one by one they were amazed to find that Hans could tap out the correct answer.

Of course, Hans' fame spread when the results of the commission were known. There were still skeptics, however, and within a few months another commission investigated Van Osten's claims. This commission, after a series of extraordinary experiments, reversed the position of the earlier investigative body. They found that Hans could only answer questions to which the questioners themselves knew the right answer. Hans was able to detect subtle cues from the questioner—a tiny forward motion of the head to start and a raised eyebrow or inaudible sign to stop—and was thereby able to get the right answers. Surprisingly, even when questioners knew they were giving Hans silent cues, they could not prevent their display. Such unconscious cues were, in this case, impossible to consciously control.[5]

The expectations of those who questioned Hans affected their behavior in ways of which they were completely unaware. Interestingly, their expectations were communicated in their unwilling signals to stop and start tapping. Clever Hans was a sensitive observer—and a smart horse.

## COMMUNICATING EXPECTATIONS

The implications of this incident are great. If we really want to understand what goes on between people and how a manager can positively influence others, we must also concentrate on nonverbal responses. This means that, besides the nonverbal messages we send to others, we must also be aware of their nonverbal messages to us. Communication encompasses nonverbal messages and responses as well as words.

Communication can best be understood as a system wherein all parts, verbal and nonverbal, are related and influence one another. To better understand interpersonal behavior, we must look at ongoing patterns, not just at isolated pieces of a message. We are always communicating, and we are always influencing the behavior of others around us. Thus, we are, in part, both molding the behavior of others through our expectations and actions and being molded by other's expectations and actions. The process is interactive.

Cornell researcher William Whyte, while studying the behavior of people in groups, noticed the significant effects of such interactive expectations. Whyte in particular observed the behavior of members of a close-knit bowling group over a considerable period of time. He found that the group, and especially its leaders, "knew" how well a person was going to bowl on a given night. In fact, each person usually performed as expected. On certain nights when the group "knew" that a person would do well, that person generally did. On other evenings, the group's expectation of a "bad night" yielded bad scores. The group's expectations, and particularly the leaders', were a major influence in whether each person did well on a particular night.[6]

None of us likes to be proved wrong. Consequently, we will sometimes go to great lengths to be sure that any predictions, silent or otherwise, do in fact come true. Sweeney was convinced of his own ability to teach George Johnson how to run a computer and was unwilling to accept the results of an IQ test that suggested he might be wrong. Perhaps the encouragement and support offered by those who were seen as leaders on the bowling team to those who were expected to do well on a given night helped them to do so by increasing their motivation and decreasing their anxiety. The confidence of individual group members was enhanced because of their leaders' confidence in them.

## COMMUNICATING CONFIDENCE

The reason why those who possess a high degree of self-confidence are able to influence others in this way is because their own sense of personal security is not violated in interpersonal exchanges. These people feel neither threatened nor insecure when others do well, because their own self-evaluations are positive. In work settings, when such people are supervisors, they are influential because they project to the workers the same confidence they have in themselves. Thus, they are able to enhance the self-confidence of other employees and thereby increase their overall productive capacity.

These supervisory expectations do not totally define other workers' self-confidence. But they do define, to a considerable extent, the things most employees feel comfortable about doing on the job. In other words, it lets certain people, who say they otherwise wouldn't do it, be assertive, or ask for assistance, or try out a new idea. As one manager said, positive supervisory and managerial expectations "help me to put on my act, to get my play presented." For many employees, managerial expectations also determine which act to put on, which play to present.

## Testing the self-fulfilling prophecy

This may explain the success of three formal tests of the self-fulfilling prophecy in industrial settings. In one study, Kansas State University professor Albert King, with no previous knowledge of any shop personnel, randomly picked the names of several welder trainees and told their supervisor that these trainees showed a high aptitude for welding. King actually knew nothing of their aptitude or ability. Months later, he found that these workers had learned their jobs faster, produced more in an average day, and were absent fewer times than their peers. Somehow the supervisor of these employees, whose names had been picked out of a hat, was able to convince them that they could succeed at welding. And succeed they did.[7]

In another study, a large number of new female employees first underwent a series of preemployment tests. The foremen who were asked to supervise these women were told that certain of the new employees had done remarkably well on the preemployment exams, while others had scored quite poorly. In reality, what the foremen were told had no relationship to the actual performance of the applicants. After several months, the production records of each new person was reviewed. The records indicated that the productivity of those who had been identified as scoring well on the initial exams was substantially higher than any of the others. Likewise, the records of those who had been identified as scoring poorly on the initial tests showed lower than average performance. Interestingly, the actual pre-employment tests, which were designed to measure intelligence and manual dexterity, also showed no relationship to their individual production output. This result could only be interpreted as another self-fulfilling prophecy.[8]

A third test of the effects of an interpersonal self-fulfilling prophecy has been reported by Sterling Livingston, a former professor at the Harvard Business School. Livingston reports that a district manager of a large insurance company decided to put his top performers in the same unit and then assigned them to work under the most capable of the assistant managers in the district. The district manager then asked this group to produce two-thirds of the total premium volume achieved by the *entire* district the year before. The district manager's plan worked. The top agents produced as expected and the overall district's performance improved about 40%. Although the productivity of these agents did improve dramatically and stayed at high levels, the performance of those who were not considered to have any chance of reaching a certain sales level actually declined. The district manager's expectations largely determined the performance of his best *and his worst* agents.[9]

The influence of one person's expectations on another person's behavior is not, of course, a business discovery. In fact, the first observation of this effect appears to have occurred in ancient times. George Bernard Shaw chose the name Pygmalion as the title for his play from a Greek myth, which tells of a sculptor by that name who carved a statue of a beautiful woman that was subsequently brought to life. Pygmalion's longing for the woman whose image he had carved was so powerful that Eros, the god of love, gave the statue life, thereby fulfilling Pygmalion's expectations for such a woman. Thus, the Pygmalion effect has sometimes been used to describe the self-fulling prophecy.

That same reason is behind the title *Pygmalion in the Classroom*, by Robert Rosenthal, a Harvard psychologist, and Lenore Jacobsen, a San Francisco school teacher. Their book details the results of experiments with interpersonal self-fulfilling prophecies in a school system. In it, Rosenthal and Jacobsen describe an elementary school in which students are tested at the beginning of each year and then placed in a fast, medium, or slow activity grouping. The researchers picked the names of sixty-five students from the first through the sixth grades and told their teachers that they were intellectual "bloomers," meaning that on their own these students would demonstrate remarkable growth during the school year. The tests scores of these children, however, did not indicate such growth possibilities. In fact, the students' names were actually chosen from a random pile of those who had *not* distinguished themselves by their test scores.

The researchers found one year later that the average IQ of the students who had been identified as "bloomers" had increased almost four points more than that of their classmates. In the earlier grades the gains were even more dramatic, with the "bloomers" increases being more than twice the increases of their peers. The "bloomers" had indeed "bloomed."

Rosenthal and Jacobsen conclude that it was not so much *what* the teachers said or did that communicated their high expectations as much as *how* they said and did things. By their facial expressions, postures, and touch, they communicated to the bloomers that they expected improved intellectual performance. In addition, the researchers indicate that the teachers watched their special children more closely, and this greater attentiveness led to rapid reinforcement of correct responses and a consequent increase in these pupils' learning and achievement. Their encouragement and support undoubtedly had a favorable effect on the "bloomers' " motivation.

The "bloomers" were, no doubt, excited to have such attention, especially since it did not carry recrimination. They were able to try out new ideas, ask questions, and get help because they knew that they would receive a favorable response from someone whose role represented authority and achievement. Their confidence and self-respect were heightened, because someone who was important to them considered their strivings worthwhile and their accomplishments significant, however small they might be in reality.[10]

## ROLE MODELING

We are always building on models and heroes—people who are important to us. As we gain new experiences, we incorporate some of the values and perspectives of people who are close to us. We take a part of them and add it to ourselves, particularly the expectations that we pick up from those we consider significant. That's why managers can exert such a powerful influence on others; those whom they supervise are probably modelling themselves on their bosses, learning from them and fulfilling their expectations, however subtly or unknowlingly such expectations may be conveyed.

It is highly unlikely that employees will substantially change any basic personality structures or patterns of psychological defenses, but they may drastically change their orientation toward people in various situations. We all learn to conduct ourselves somewhat differently in different situations and for different roles. The behavior we exhibit at work usually varies from that exhibited at home; our spouses and bosses, our peers and our children, our doctors and door-to-door salesmen all see different images. Almost intuitively, we size up a situation, determine what is expected of us in that situation, and act accordingly.

Moreover, in the continued presence of someone we respect, we also learn to act out new images of ourselves. We acquire new attitudes and values, new competencies, and new ways of conducting ourselves in interpersonal situations through social interaction. The research evidence for the proposition that we pick up and incorporate the attitudes and values of people who are important to us is quite impressive. The evidence suggests that people do what the people who are personally important to them think they should do. Basically, it comes from two sources, Hawthorne effect studies, and placebo effect studies.

### Hawthorne effect

The Hawthorne effect derives its name from research done more than 50 years ago by two Harvard Business School professors,

Fritz Roethlisberger and Elton Mayo, at the Hawthorne plant of the Western Electric Company. The researchers began by studying the effects of such factors as lighting, heat, fatigue, and physical layout on productivity. A group of workers was selected for the first experiment, which was aimed at identifying the effects of lighting on output. It was found that as illumination was increased in the test group production also increased. Furthermore, when the lighting intensity was decreased below the original levels, it was found that output *still* improved. Not until the intensity of illumination had been decreased to the equivalent of ordinary moonlight was there any appreciable decline in output.[11]

The lighting study showed that positive results in productivity can be achieved independently of the content of changes that may be implemented. Thus, the Hawthorne effect is used to describe the results of an experimental effect or change program where positive results are related to the employees' feeling special and believing in the wisdom of the experimenter or change agent. The Hawthorne effect also suggests that people who feel especially selected for a certain effect will tend to show it.

Eaton Industries, headquartered in Cleveland, Ohio, has actively tried to use this idea to improve the quality of worklife and the output of workers at their new factories. Plant management personnel indicate that what they are trying to do is to "bottle" the Hawthorne effect. This is done by allowing workers to be involved in making changes in their work routine and job layout. Since workers have an active voice in changes in equipment or personnel policies that affect them, they tend to be more committed to making those changes work. The results have been quite impressive when this approach has been taken at newer plant locations. Not only are absenteeism and turnover much lower at these plant locations than at other locations in the company, but start-up costs and output are also much better than at the more traditional plants.[12]

David McClelland, chairman of the Department of Social Relations at Harvard University and a prominent management consultant, also believes that the Hawthorne effect can be

"bottled," especially in attempting to change business procedures or managerial practices. He maintains that belief in the
possibility and desirability of change are tremendously influential in changing a person. So he uses the authority of his own
research findings, the suggestive power of membership in an
experimental group, and the prestige of his university position
when working with managers to establish his personal base as an
authority and utilize the power of the Hawthorne effect. His
record of success would indicate that what he does certainly
works.[13]

These examples serve to illustrate the basis of the
Hawthorne effect and establish the validity of the interpersonal
self-fulfilling prophecy. They are essentially two different terms
of the same phenomenon. People tend to do or believe what is
expected of them, especially when the person holding an
expectation is a prestigious source.

## Placebo effect

Physicians have long recognized that their own ability to inspire
the patient's trust and expectation of healing partially determines the success of treatment. At times, doctors have resorted
to the use of a placebo, a pharmacologically inert substance,
such as a sugar pill or a water injection, to relieve a patient's dis-
tress. Studying the reactions of patients to placebos is another
means of studying the effects of expectations on behavior.

Evidence that placebos can have marked physiological
effects and can even heal tissue damage is impressive. The
placebo treatment of warts, for example, by painting them with a
brightly colored dye and telling the patient that the wart will be
gone by the time the color wears off, is as effective in wart
removal as any other treatment, including surgical excision.[14]
Placebo treatment can also activate healing of more severely
damaged tissue. In an experimental study of patients hos-
pitalized with bleeding peptic ulcers, 70% showed "excellent
results lasting over a period of one year" when a doctor gave
them an injection of distilled water and assured them that it was
a new medicine that would cure the condition.[15]

Placebos have also been shown to be effective in causing the remission of cancer, curing colds, and eliminating a variety of other maladies. Placebos produce an effect based solely on a patient's confidence in the physician. This resembles the "Hello–Goodbye" effect in psychotherapy. Studies have been conducted showing that patients with emotional distresses who merely have brief contact with a prestigious medical authority improve almost as much as those who get prolonged therapy.[16]

None of these reported results are intended to demonstrate that many people are hypochondriacs or that most ailments are simply "all in your head." Such a conclusion would be erroneous. Rather, these studies supply more evidence that belief in a physician's ability is an important element of that person's ability to heal. Confidence in others and in ourselves leads to success.

## BUILDING SELF-CONFIDENCE

Someone who believes that gaining self-confidence is difficult will find that it *is* so. Self-fulfilling prophecies are most effective regarding what we think we can do. Yet, believing that we can be more self-confident is only the beginning. We must do something that actively demonstrates to our satisfaction that we are worthy, capable, and competent. Once we have a stockpile of personal accomplishments and a baseline of self-regard, the recognition of others can sustain us and encourage us to do better and better. External affirmation without internal self-valuing, however, does *not* nourish us and help us grow. The following are a variety of exercises that can help people become more self-confident and better able to use the self-fulfilling prophecy as a managerial tool.

### Goal setting

Successfully accomplishing a difficult task builds self-confidence. So the first thing to decide is what you want to accomplish. Write down three long-range goals, which might take a year or more to accomplish, and three short-range goals, which you can reach in a week or a month. Use the following guidelines to help select your goals.

1. *Conceivable.* You must first be able to picture yourself having already accomplished the goal and then be able to identify clearly what the first step must be to start off.

2. *Believable.* You must believe that you can achieve the goal. Has someone you know accomplished this goal? Are you able to use that person as an example or role model of the things you must do to reach the goal?

3. *Controllable.* If your goal includes the involvement of someone else, you should get their agreement to participate or to share resources.

4. *Measurable.* Your goal must be stated so that it is measurable in time and quantity. You must have some way to know when you have reached your goal.

5. *Desirable.* Your goal should be something you want to do. It is true that you can do almost anything you want, but you cannot do everything you want. You must choose. Your goal must be capable of moving you to action.

Write down where you are now, how you are going to get where you are going, and when you'll know that you've arrived. You might want to fill out a form, such as the one shown on the next page, and keep it in a place where you can refer to it often.

### Keeping a journal

The more you learn about yourself, the more likely you are to find out what you like, what you want, and what makes you feel good about yourself. By keeping a journal you are forced to become a good observer. This can help you to become sensitive to what works and why in your interactions with others. You can come to see yourself and others more clearly, and this skill can enable you to be more successful with others. This success, like all others, is a building block for your own self-confidence. By

| Where do I want to go? | Where am I now? | How am I going to get there? | When will I know that I've arrived? |
|---|---|---|---|
|  |  |  |  |

feeling that you can understand and exert some control over things that go on around you, you emerge more confident and purposeful.

Keeping a journal forces you to become chroniclers of events. It is amazing how much we have to relearn simply because we don't take the time to catalogue our memories. One way to keep a journal is to keep a manila folder for "new learnings" in your desk. At a convenient time, say at the end or beginning of a day, try to indicate what you might have learned about yourself by completing some of the following sentences.

> I learned that I _____.
> I relearned that I _____.
> I think I would be more effective if I _____.
> I would like to be more (less) _____.

## Imaging

Dorothy Susskind, a professor at the City University of New York, maintains that an effective way to increase self-confidence is to conjure up a picture in your mind of the kind of person you would like to be and then work toward that ideal. This process is termed "imaging." She advocates using the following steps.

1. Write a description of the person you would like to be. Writing it down is important; so is being specific.

2. Make a checklist to help you periodically inventory your progress.

3. Realize that you must give up some things in order to get others. Be aware of the choices you make and their congruence with your ideal.

4. Work on things that are within your control. Do not rely too heavily on things that depend on someone else's evaluation.

5. Ask yourself frequently: "How would my idealized person act in this situation?" Ask this question especially of situations that concern you.

## Rehearsing

Something that has helped athletes gain more confidence while getting ready for an athletic event is doing a behavioral rehearsal. Jean-Claude Killy, a three-time Olympic gold medal winner, reported that once he did not even have a chance to take a practice run on the particular ski course before the event. His only preparation was to ski it mentally several times. He won, and later reported that it was one of his best races.

This same technique can help you approach any situation with more confidence. You can mentally practice problem situations before they occur or even role play the situation in your mind. What should you say or do, and how should you go about saying or doing it? By practicing beforehand you are more likely to feel in command of whatever transpires.

Former Associate Justice of the Supreme Court Learned Hand, who was known as a master conversationalist, used this technique to prepare for every social event he attended. Before leaving his house, he would make a mental inventory of questions to ask the various guests he might meet. Then, when he arrived at the party or social gathering and did meet someone new, all he needed to do was recall his list of questions.

## Making collages

All of us have symbols that represent the person we think we are. The kind of car you drive, the brand of cigarette you smoke, the magazines you read, and the music you listen to all symbolize what you think about yourself. You can learn much about yourself by carefully examining those symbols. More important, you can do much to increase your confidence by creatively manipulating the symbols that you choose to represent you.

Get a copy of as many different magazines as you can; select magazines that are filled with pictures. Cut out the pictures that represent your personal strengths. Be good to yourself and give yourself the benefit of any doubt. Paste them on a large piece of poster paper or thin cardboard. Include as many different aspects of you as you can. Then, display this collage in a location where you will see it often and be reminded of your personal strengths.

## SUMMARY

Expectations of a person's behavior strongly affect what that person does. When we hold assumptions regarding someone else's behavior, our expectations can subtly but powerfully serve as an interpersonal self-fulfilling prophecy. This fact can be observed and has been documented in a variety of settings. In a business setting, it is possible for managers to create high performance expectations and therefore get better results from those whom they supervise.

Such expectations depend on more than mere wishing and must be more than the power of positive thinking. Managers must realize that how they treat others communicates their real expectations more convincingly than what they may say. Moreover, their ability to get results depends on their own self-confidence, the confidence and self-esteem they build in others, and the confidence that others have in them.

Something is going on in the minds of effective managers that is foreign to their less-effective counterparts. Effective managers seem to be more aware of who they are and what they want and, consequently, are not required to look to others for direction and guidance. They are not loners; they enjoy being with people and enjoy recognition. But the praise and status that others bestow on effective managers serve to confirm their own self-images. Since status and praise do not create this image, they do not depend on them.

The high expectations that effective managers have of others are simply an extension of the expectations they have of themselves. What managers believe about themselves, including their ability to perform required tasks well, powerfully influences what they believe about others and, in turn, what others believe about them. If managers can develop self-confidence, they can develop confidence in others and can learn to communicate their expectations in such a way that they will become self-fulfilling prophecies.

## REFERENCES

1. H. H. Kelley, "The Warm-Cold Variable in First Impressions of People," *Journal of Personality*, Vol. 18, 1950, pp. 431–439.

2. Rensis Likert, *New Patterns of Management*. New York: McGraw-Hill, 1961.

3. Cited in Robert Rosenthal and Lenore Jacobsen, *Pygmalion in the Classroom*. New York: Holt, Rinehart & Winston, 1968.

4. Douglas MacGregor, *The Professional Manager*. New York: McGraw-Hill, 1967.

5. Cited in Philip G. Zimbardo and Floyd L. Ruch, *Psychology and Life*. Glenview, Ill.: Scott Foresman, 1975.

6. William F. Whyte, *Street Corner Society*. Chicago: University of Chicago Press, 1955.

7. Albert S. King, "Expectation Effects in Organizational Change," *Administrative Science Quarterly*, Vol. 19, 1974, pp. 221–230.

8. C. S. Raben and R. J. Klimoski, "The Effects of Expectations Upon Task Performance as Moderated by Levels of Self-Esteem," *Journal of Vocational Behavior*, Vol. 3, 1973, pp. 475–483.

9. J. Sterling Livingston, "Pygmalion in Management," *Harvard Business Review*, July–August 1969, pp. 81–89.

10. Rosenthal and Jacobsen, *Pygmalion in the Classroom*.

11. Fritz Roethlisberger and William J. Dickson, *Management and the Worker*. Cambridge: Harvard University Press, 1939.

12. Donald Scobel, "Doing Away with the Factory Blues," *Harvard Business Review*, November–December 1975, pp. 133–142.

13. David C. McClelland, "Toward a Theory of Motive Acquisition," *American Psychologist*, Vol. 20, 1965, pp. 321–333.

14. Jefferson Fish, *Placebo Therapy: A Practical Guide to Social Influence in Psychotherapy*. San Francisco: Jossey-Bass, 1973.

15. Ibid.

16. Jerome Frank, *Persuasion and Healing*. Baltimore: Johns Hopkins University Press, 1961.

# CHAPTER 6
# IMPROVING MOTIVATION
# AND PRODUCTIVITY

Snoopy: Yesterday I was a dog. Today I'm a dog.
Tomorrow I'll probably still be a dog. There's just so little
hope of advancement.

From *You're A Good Man Charlie Brown* by Clark Gessner

More and more people joining the workforce today are looking for jobs that not only make money but also have meaning.
According to Daniel Katz and Robert Kahn of the Institute for
Social Research at the University of Michigan, the one thing that
people particularly want from their job besides adequate pay is
the opportunity for purposeful action and self-advancement.
When that is not present, individual motivation wanes. When it is
present, people are willing to put forth the kind of effort that will
increase the productivity of the enterprise that employs them.[1]

People always seem to have an astonishing amount of energy for activities that really excite them. We have undoubtedly seen many who are willing to spend long hours or take special precautions to ensure that certain projects are completed correctly and on time. Why can't that energy be harnessed more often? Why can't it be tapped more fully?

It can. It takes the kind of energy and commitment that managers often reserve for production or financial problems. It takes the proper application of a few guidelines that demand consistent application. But it can be done, and it can make a difference.

## WHAT IS MOTIVATION?

Some people think of motivation as a rather mysterious ingredient that is put into individuals to make them run, as gasoline is put into a car. Consequently, they do all kinds of things to try and keep the tank full. Motivation, however, isn't a fuel that gets injected into someone. Rather, it is an individual attribute that is a product of several social forces. John W. Gardner, former Secretary of Health, Education, and Welfare, says that these forces include patterns of child rearing, the tone of the educational system, presence or absence of opportunity, the tendency of the society to release or smother available energy, and social attitudes toward dedication and commitment.[2]

Undoubtedly, motivation is a function of all these social forces. They all contribute to a person's willingness to put forth effort in order to perform a task. They all suggest, moreover, that motivation is not something a person is born with or without, but rather is something that can be developed and enhanced. In addition, these forces suggest certain things that can be done to get someone more motivated. They point to the kind of conditions that must exist in an organization in order to have motivated people.

In the past, managers have taken three basic approaches to tapping this reserve of employee energy and getting employee commitment. The oldest approach was quite simple: "We'll *make* them do it." This assumed that people did things because they were told to, so all that was needed to get employees motivated was to tell them they had to work hard. This approach did work for a while, but unions and industrial engineers came along and both said to the workers, in effect, "This is how hard you are supposed to work." Of course, the quotas of the industrial engineer and the union may not have agreed, but the result of each was to limit the amount of work an executive could tell an employee to produce.

Society changed and so did many jobs. The rise of automation made an employee's willingness to do a good job almost as important as the ability to do a good job. So a second approach was tried, which was basically, "We'll make them *want* to do it." This worked with some employees, but others could see that it was little more than a gimmicky version of "We'll make them do it." Besides, employees who were now coming into the workforce at all levels were generally better educated than their predecessors, and they wanted reasons for doing things. Just being told what to do was not enough anymore, regardless of how the instructions were clothed.

Thus, a third approach was tried out, which said, "We'll make them *happy doing* it." This approach said that a satisfied worker was a productive worker, so workers should be kept satisfied in order to be kept motivated. Although this approach sounded most promising, research showed that it just didn't work.[3] In fact, satisfaction seems to be what an employee feels after doing a good job and is not an incentive to work hard.

So what does work? What can a manager do in order to get employee motivation? The only workable approach is simply this: "We'll make them *responsible*." Managers must set up and maintain conditions that allow employees to be responsible and to look to the executive as a source of help. This approach replaces externally imposed dictums with internally set reasons for doing things. There is no other way to get an employee to do something willingly and with personal commitment. There is no other way to get to the kind of motivation that affects performance.

Every organization provides people with a sense of what is expected of them. If the organization is lax in its demands, people will exert little effort. However, if much is expected of people, then chances are the people will expect much of themselves. It is possible to create an atmosphere that encourages effort and vigorous performance. It is possible to establish a climate where people want to fulfill the expectations of those who guide and direct them.

One way to begin assessing the climate of an organization is through a questionnaire. This will give a clear picture of current organizational practices and indicate as well how the employees feel about them. By locating specific problem areas in this way, a manager is in a better position to develop a plan of action for improving conditions in order to foster motivation. An example of a questionnaire that can be useful in identifying such problem areas is given in Appendix I at the end of this chapter.

## MOTIVATION TECHNIQUES

There are some specific actions that a manager can take once problem areas have been located. Those actions that can positively affect employee motivation include:

- setting challenging performance goals;
- allowing employee discretion in achieving objectives;
- ensuring adequate resources;
- creating direct communication links between producers and users;
- being consistent and fair;
- giving feedback based on performance;
- providing recognition and opportunity;
- sharing information on problems and successes with employees.

Each of these eight steps describe action levers that can be pushed to get the increase in productivity that an increase in motivation generally yields. These eight dimensions indicate *what* must be done to improve motivation. Now let's see *how* to use each action lever.

## Setting challenging goals

A research project undertaken at General Electric concluded that employees tend to be more satisfied with their jobs as more difficult goals are set in their work area, provided they are allowed to participate in the goal-setting process.[7] To set effective goals, a manager must provide employees with the guidelines mentioned in Chapter 5, which state that goals must be conceivable, believable, controllable, measurable, and desirable.

One executive put these guidelines into practice by distributing them to each employee he supervised and asking them individually to set goals, outline what they needed from him to accomplish their goals, and be prepared to discuss their plans within ten days. Then he called a meeting of all employees and had them all describe their ideas. Not only did every employee accomplish those goals, but more challenging goals were set each time this process was repeated. The executive found that peer pressure could be used to provide a better control mechanism for goal attainment than could his own admonitions.

Another variation of this technique was used by a district manager in an oil company. He called members of his work group together and indicated that he wanted to improve the overall output of the unit. He then passed out the guidelines for goal setting, asked the group to come up with goals they were committed to and to give him a copy of them, and left the room. Without the boss's influence, the group came up with some creative goals to which they all agreed. Each goal was realized.

Sometimes the success of such goal setting is thought to be due to employee participation. Although such involvement is very useful in many cases, the real key to success is the fact that goals were explicit. This enabled the employees to use them as criteria in setting priorities for their own work. Not having specific goals in an organizational unit is like having a foot race with an unannounced and unmarked finish line. Consequently, the participants don't know whether to jog or to sprint. One of the purest acts of leadership is this process of setting goals and getting others to work toward them. It is a key to both motivation and productivity.

## Allowing employee discretion in achieving objectives

Too often managers tend to govern activity instead of controlling direction. They get caught up in what George Odiorne, Dean of the School of Business at the University of Massachusetts, calls "the activity trap." Odiorne says that in an activity oriented organization it is possible to improve competence without improving output. This is because people are getting better and better at activities that do not count. More over, this activity orientation stifles motivation because there is no room for individual creativity or innovation.[8]

Allowing employees to have some say regarding various work methods is one way for a manager to communicate the belief that the employees are responsible. By removing some controls and delegating more authority (while still retaining accountability), a manager can directly enhance employee motivation.

Frederick Herzberg, a well-known consultant and professor of Management at the University of Utah, has reported a situation in which allowing employees to have more control over work methods paid off very well. The subjects of his study were stockholder correspondents employed by a large corporation. Procedural changes included allowing correspondents to sign most letters, making proofreading their responsibility instead of the supervisor's and holding each correspondent personally responsible for the quality and accuracy of letters. A shareholder service index was constructed to measure the effects of these changes, and the results indicated that performance had consistently improved since the start of the project. Moreover, a questionnaire designed to measure the motivation of the correspondents found that increases had also occurred in this area since the changes in work methods had been made.[9]

In 1964, *Time* magazine asked then Ford Motor Company "whiz-kid" Lee Iacocca the secret of his very successful managerial style. "How do I manage?" replied Iacocca. "At the beginning of every quarter, I sit down with every manager who works for me and we talk about 'what are you going to produce for me during the coming year.' That's his commitment." Iacocca went on to emphasize that he then acts as a resource to each manager, but doesn't meddle in the manager's methods. He sets the pace and keeps the focus on direction and lets each manager be creative in approach.

Once a manager is convinced that an assignment has been appropriately explained and fully understood, the employees should use their own methods for achieving the project's desired results. Creativity suffers under close and controlling supervision. Theodore Roosevelt said it this way: "The best executive is the one who has sense enough to pick good men to do what he wants done, and self-restraint enough to keep from meddling with them while they do it."

A system of managing that is centered around getting everyone committed to goals and allowing discretion in achieving them is both functional and developmental. It makes money while at the same time fostering a climate that permits people to grow. It is effective because it builds on people's natural desire for achievement and success.

There are many signs indicating that the carrot-and-stick techniques for governing activity are ineffective. They may get movement, but they do not get motivation. In order to get others motivated, a manager must provide on-the-job opportunities for people to succeed and let that success act as an incentive for improvement. It can be powerful, and it is probably the only way to get lasting commitment from employees, not just their short-term compliance.

### Ensuring adequate resources

Sometimes "motivational programs" are constructed and launched in order to counteract a decline in employee output. In many of these cases, however, the remedies for the problems are actually simpler than they may initially appear. A lack of motivation and a decline in output may be directly attributed to a simple lack of adequate resources. Let me illustrate.

In a large manufacturing concern, a consultant was called in to assess the reasons for a continuing decline in productivity at a particular plant and for an increase in union militancy. Even though interviews with workers produced such complaints as inadequate pay, poor supervision, and the like, he continued to feel that these were only symptoms of a more basic problem. Finally, he discovered the real cause of discontent and lack of motivation. He discovered that, because there was so much paperwork and delay involved in going through formal channels to get materials and tools from the company storehouse, the employees were stealing from the warehouse in order to do their work. The frustration produced by internal bureaucracy plus the anxiety raised by the possibility of getting caught and being fired were not incentives to work hard.

One characteristic of jobs where employees are highly motivated is a provision for adequate resources. In many situations, this characteristic can be built into a job by giving employees the opportunity to schedule their own work and have control over the supply of resources they need. This does not mean that they set the deadline; they set their pace to meet it.

One of the more serious complaints executives have of employees is that they are indifferent to costs. Responsible cost control, however, can occur only when someone truly has responsibility for costs. Often, by providing employees with mini-budgets for their operations, managers succeed in having them take responsibility for costs. What this amounts to is putting cost and profit centers as far down in an organization as possible. There are few instances when cost center in simplified form cannot be used at an individual or team level. An example of such action occurred when design engineers at one plant were given the authority to spend all the money allocated to a particular project. All administrative limits, such as approval for expenditures of more than a set amount, were removed. As a result, the costs declined and came more in line with figures management considered realistic.

### Creating direct communication links

Another characteristic of a motivating work environment is the opportunity for employees who create a product or provide a service to develop relationships with clients. A client relationship is one in which regular and direct communication about the quality of the product or service occurs between producer and user. Too often in many organizations, employees are isolated from the people they are supposed to serve. To them, "customers" are either a sterile quote or a multiple layer of committees. The wage employees are merely told what specifications are required in order to meet standards; the staff people must go through "the proper channels" before their ideas are heard. Usually, neither group can find out what the customers want or how satisfied they are with the product or service.

Let me give two examples of a direct producer-customer communication link and its benefits. At an electronics firm, management was unhappy with the performance of workers on an important subassembly. The operations managers then modified the system so that the unit was assigned to work directly with the main assemblers, who received the product next. Team meetings were held so that worker could talk directly to worker. The result has been an increase in cooperation between the two units and a decrease in the reject rate for units produced by the subassembly group.[10]

In another situation, executives at a credit card billing center were concerned about the number of errors that their keypunchers made and the number of customer complaints that were received about incorrect billings. In an effort to reverse this trend, management assigned keypunchers to handle bills coming only from certain geographical locations. Moreover, each keypuncher was assigned a service number, so that complaints could be passed directly from the customer to the keypuncher who had processed that customer's bill. In this way, not only was accountability increased, but a producer-user communication link was also established. This action resulted in a decline in customer complaints and an increase in worker satisfaction with the job.

The reason why these direct communications links positively affected productivity is that they made the employees directly responsible for their work. All the employees saw what impact their performance has on others, and this accountability caused them to be more concerned about doing a good job. In each case, the employees who had their jobs changed felt they were not just working for "the company" now, but also serving other people.

## Being consistent and fair

One of the things that employees at all levels have repeatedly requested is fair and consistent treatment on the job. This can significantly affect how much effort they extend or whether they extend any effort at all. But how can you tell whether you are being consistent and fair? Consider these two executives, Don and Betty, who are in the same large corporation.

Don is a very friendly person who spends a lot of time talking with those he supervises. He prides himself on being warm and sensitive to the needs of others. If an employee were to ask for time off to take care of a personal problem, Don might worry about breaking the rules, but probably give in anyway.

Betty, on the other hand, enjoys being the boss and encourages others to do their job well. Although amiable, she is considerably less warm than Don. She has high personal standards and a penchant for meeting deadlines. If an employee asks for time off because of a personal problem, Betty would suggest using some vacation time or taking an unpaid leave of absence.

Who is the better boss? Many people might quickly choose generous, friendly Don. But research conducted by David McClelland, Professor of Psychology at Harvard, shows that nice guys like Don can make poor bosses.[11] Compared to Betty, he gets less work out of his people and creates lower morale. The reason for such poor results, McClelland reports, is that the desire to be liked leads people like Don into wishy-washy decisions. Because they want to be liked by everyone, they cater to the happiness of particular individuals and ignore the well-being of the entire working group. By making exceptions to company rules, they violate the principle of fairness.

When managers bend the rules for particular individuals, other employees are often alienated. The failure to treat people equally destroys the workers' faith in the system. The inconsistent decisions may also make subordinates feel powerless to control events. Whether they do well or poorly, they don't know what to expect next. This does not mean that executives who do well are authoritarian, but simply that they are consistent.

There is a fine line between operating consistently and merely going by the book. One way to tell how well employees are doing is to look at results. Are employees involved in their work? Do they feel the sense of freedom and security that comes from sharing in rules everyone lives by? Or do they feel that no decision can be made without consulting "the book"? Do they feel hemmed in? Do they feel a sense of rigidity that suggests some rules are either out-of-date or unreasonable? These are important questions, and their answers are equally important.

## Giving performance feedback

The importance of on-the-job feedback is almost universally recognized. Everyone realizes that good job performance must be noticed if it is to continue, and poor job performance must be corrected if it is to change. However, the application of this idea in most organizations works against sustaining the motivation of employees. Typically, feedback is given in such a way that the personal satisfaction or dissatisfaction to be derived from work behavior is denied the employee.

For specific examples of feedback that does and does not enhance motivation, consider the case of a worker who successfully completes a complicated task in an efficient manner. If the boss says, "I'm pleased that you did such a good job; keep it up, that's the kind of work I like to see done," who is being rewarded? Not the worker—the boss! The boss is the one who is happy and has, in essence, complimented only himself. If, on the other hand, the boss notices a job well done and says "My, that's fine workmanship. You must feel a real sense of accomplishment," the employee is reinforced instead. By recognizing performance in this way, the employee's own feelings of satisfaction are reinforced and the internal, personal generator is lubricated.

Most managers are aware of the potential for positive impact when they give feedback to employees. They know that any message affecting people's feelings about themselves — verbal or nonverbal, formal or informal — is going to have consequences for future interpersonal relations and performance. The best impact, moreover, will be achieved when good performance is noticed by reinforcing the employee's own feelings of satisfaction and accomplishment. Poor performance can be corrected in the same way — by noticing it and simply acknowledging that the employee is undoubtedly personally dissatisfied.

Sometimes, however, that is the only feedback some employees get. If so, they may realize that they are not doing a good job, but may not know how to improve. If this is the case, training is necessary. And the best way for people to learn is by getting some of the positive feedback just described.

Managers will notice increases in motivation and performance when they reinforce the employees' innate satisfaction from a job well done. Mistakes are less likely to occur when such feedback is consistently given because people naturally want to succeed and they are reinforced for doing so. Those mistakes that do happen are more likely to be learned from rather than repeated in the future. It is the nearest thing to a performance insurance policy that is available.

### Providing recognition and opportunity

Everyone wants opportunities for purposeful action and self-advancement. Jobs are important not only in and of themselves but also in terms of the status and recognition they provide. One of the first questions someone typically asks of a stranger is "What do you do?" Since the kind of job a person has is the major means by which self-esteem is maintained, it is also the major means by which motivation can be enhanced.

The amount of opportunity people see in their jobs has a direct relationship to their job performance, reports Rosabeth Kanter, a Yale University researcher. She has found that people with fewer opportunities tend to lower their aspirations, become less engaged with or committed to work, and behave in ways that usually make others see them as being unsuitable for promotion.

Having more opportunities has the opposite effect—that of encouraging people to adopt attitudes and behaviors that will further the interests of the company to which they belong.[12]

A similar situation, in which increasing the opportunities available to a group of employees increased performance, took place in a large chemical company. In a research laboratory, technicians were given the responsibility for documenting research reports and for training laboratory assistants. Those who developed proficiencies in analyzing and evaluating data were assigned as apprentices to the research scientists and allowed to develop professional competencies. Those who showed an aptitude for training others were given increased managerial responsibilities and allowed to become supervisors. By simply removing the lid from advancement opportunities and creating dual career paths, the performance of the lab technicians changed dramatically.

It is easy to provide recognition and opportunities to an organization's superstars. Such people usually get the status and recognition they deserve. Yet, the performers who are not quite as good as the best tend to go unnoticed. What is done for them? Unfortunately, very little is done for them in many companies, so they often do less than they are capable of doing.

## Sharing information

A vital ingredient in the success of any organized enterprise is the open sharing of information. Communication implies developing an understanding between a sender and a receiver by allowing both the chance to speak and to listen. If executives sit down with those they supervise and share their thoughts about the successes and problems that confront all of them, it can be a real boost to motivation.

Many managers share few of their own feelings or ideas with others. Directing, ordering, talking, or commanding are all quite different from sharing. Sharing is the process of getting thoughts and feelings out in the open so that problems can be solved adequately and issues resolved appropriately. Such sharing results in collaborative problem solving and joint commitment. In fact, commitment is said to be a product of involvement.

At Texas Instruments, this approach has been used with remarkable results in recent years. Each executive is expected to meet monthly with all employees and review the group's accomplishments during that month. After headlining successes, the employees are asked to share problems they may have encountered in the last month. Rather than focusing on solutions, the group attempts to be problem oriented. The executive encourages them to describe the basis for the problems they've mentioned as well as any apparent consequences. In this way, mutual problem identification and definition results. The manager gets ideas on what needs improving, but is not forced to resolve the issue on the spot, being left free to gather more facts and examine the problems from other perspectives.

Why does this principle work? Most people know inside what is right and what they should do, but they are often barred from sharing responsibility. However, when they are trusted enough to hear some of the facts of a problem situation that affects them, along with some of the feelings and concerns of those in authority, they want to help. They feel honored; they want to give their best ideas and, eventually, their cooperation. This process engages people instead of disengaging them. It builds a sense of "we" and breaks down "us-them" barriers.

## IMPLEMENTING THE ACTION STEPS

Each of the eight action steps just described indicate ways in which motivation can be enhanced and productivity improved. They include what to do and how to go about each step. One more thing is important in this entire process: the executive's supporting role in implementing these action steps. What should be done to ensure true change and real increases in productivity? It is important for managers to do three things: train, commit, help.

The training process is essential when people are required to do things differently. Do they know what to do, how to do it, and why it must be done at all? Sometimes managers fall short in providing adequate training; thus, the result of their efforts to improve things is disappointing. Appropriate training not only ensures the clear understanding of what is expected but also a sense of security from knowing exactly what to do.

Getting the employee to make commitments regarding the future course of action is the next step in the process and it is just as important as training. Its success, however, hinges on a mutual agreement, not simply a shallow one-way action. Kurt Lewin, a researcher at the University of Iowa during World War II, demonstrated just how vital this phase is in getting people to change. The State Department had asked Lewin to experiment with ways to get civilians to buy nonrationed cuts of meat (such as liver, heart, and tongue) so that the choicer cuts could be sent to the soldiers overseas.

Lewin set up two experimental groups to see which conditions would most motivate housewives, to buy the nonrationed cuts. For one group, he brought in speakers who emphasized that it was the civilians' patriotic duty to buy these cuts. The speakers also described the nutritional aspects of these cuts of meat and gave out recipes detailing how to prepare meals using them. Thus, the housewives knew what to do, how to do it, and why it was important to do it. Despite these extensive lectures, only about 3% of the participants actually changed their buying habits.

In the other group, housewives were requested to participate in discussion groups dealing with such topics as food, nutrition, and the war effort. During these sessions, the participants were asked to make commitments to each other describing what they were going to do differently to support the war effort. The result? Ten times the number of lecture-group housewives changed their buying habits.[13] Making commitments made the difference.

Once a commitment is made, the last aspect of implementation is for the manager to become a source of help. This is done by making employees accountable for doing the work, but also by being available for assistance with problems when they need it. The manager provides feedback, support, and the like, but does not take over any responsibility that an employee may have. Robert Townsend, the man who made unknown Avis Rent-a-Car the best known No. 2 in the nation, quotes Chinese philosopher Lao-tzu's guiding philosophy on this point: "When the best leader's work is done the people say, 'We did it ourselves.' "[14]

## SUMMARY

There is a great deal of talk today about "giving" people pride in their work and a sense of importance or achievement. But pride and accomplishment cannot be given. People cannot be "made" to feel important. They are either valued or not valued and, in turn, they see their work as either valuable or unimportant. Service pins and other forms of recognition have meaning only when they represent some inner accomplishment. Managers need to do something about providing more and better opportunities for people at all levels in the organization and with varying abilities to achieve.

Motivation is often thought of as a personality trait, and either you have it or you don't. Often, poor performance is attributed to a person's "lack of motivation." Despite this use, motivation is more the result of work conditions that encourage employees to achieve rather than a personal characteristic. True, motivation resides within and is an individual attribute, but everyone has it, and the right combination of keys will release it.

It is not necessary to understand how people's personalities improve motivation and productivity. People are distinct, complex entities, but they are also quite similar in some very basic ways. These similarities and their effects on people should be the focus of improvement. The similarities make the difference.

An essential task incumbent on every executive is to arrange organizational conditions and methods of operation so that the proper conditions for motivation are arranged at the workplace. Most of the conditions necessary for making productive and motivated employees are easily in an executive's control. The trouble is, managers are not usually as adept at using them to improve employee output as they are in using raw materials and machines to improve material output. It may not be easy to create the conditions and practice the skills that have been described, but it will certainly be worth the effort.

# REFERENCES

1. Daniel Katz and Robert L. Kahn, *The Social Psychology of Organizations.* New York: John Wiley, 1966.

2. John W. Gardner, *Self-Renewal.* New York: Harper & Row, 1964.

3. Lyman W. Porter and Edward E. Lawler, "What Job Attitudes Tell About Motivation," *Harvard Business Review,* Organizational Development Series III. Cambridge: Harvard University Press, 1970.

4. Rensis Likert, *New Patterns of Management.* New York: McGraw-Hill, 1961.

5. Robert Rosenthal, "The Pygmalion Effect Lives," *Psychology Today,* July 1973, pp. 56–59.

6. Douglas MacGregor, *The Human Side of Enterprise.* New York: McGraw-Hill, 1961.

7. General Electric Company, *A Comparison of a Work Planning Program With the Annual Performance Appraisal Interview Approach.* Management Development and Employee Relations Services, 1964.

8. George S. Odiorne, *Management and the Activity Trap.* New York: Harper & Row, 1974.

9. Frederick Herzberg, *The Managerial Choice.* Homewood, Ill.: Richard D. Irwin, 1976.

10. J. Carroll Swart, "The Worth of Humanistic Management: Some Contemporary Examples," *Business Horizons,* June 1973, pp. 41–50.

11. David C. McClelland and David H. Burnham, "Good Guys Make Bum Bosses," *Psychology Today,* December 1975, pp. 69–70.

12. Rosabeth M. Kanter, *Men and Women of the Corporation.* New York: Basic Books, 1977.

13. Kurt Lewin, "Group Decision and Social Change," in *Readings in Social Psychology,* ed. Eleanor E. Maccoby et al. New York: Holt and Co., 1958.

14. Robert Townsend, *Up the Organization.* New York: Alfred A. Knopf, 1970.

# APPENDIX I

# SAMPLE QUESTIONNAIRE

Instructions: The purpose of this questionnaire is to discover how you feel about the functioning of your own work group. In order to do this, beside each of the statements circle the number that most typically describes how people work together. Avoid the tendency to either ignore weaknesses or downplay strengths. Then, under the *Behaviors* and *Consequences* headings, list specific examples of things you have observed that caused you to evaluate the work group as you did.

Consider the following example. Suppose that, in a meeting to discuss a problem, several people keep interrupting you in order to make their points. Instead of trying to decide why those individuals interrupted, simply describe the *behavior* (interrupting) and the *consequence* (feeling put down, shut out, etc.) that resulted. In this way, your response deals with *what* happened and *how* it affected you and others without going into *why* it happened, and it is easier to focus on ways to improve. It is important in this endeavor to view the consequences of someone else's behavior, regardless of the intent, as valid information.

## COOPERATION

1. To what degree do people work together in order to accomplish mutual tasks?

| 1 | 2 | 3 | 4 | 5 |
|---|---|---|---|---|
| Everyone really pulls together on this team. | | | | It's "every man for himself" around here. |

2. Our planning and the way we operate as a team is largely influenced by:

| 1 | 2 | 3 | 4 | 5 |
|---|---|---|---|---|
| All members of the team. | | | | One or two members of the team. |

*Behaviors*                                        *Consequences*

## LISTENING

3.  To what degree do people pay attention to what others have to say?

| 1 | 2 | 3 | 4 | 5 |
|---|---|---|---|---|
| When someone brings up an idea people take note. | | | | Some people ignore others' suggestions. |

*Behaviors*                                    *Consequences*

## VALUING

4.  To what extent are people made to feel that they are important and their work necessary?

| 1 | 2 | 3 | 4 | 5 |
|---|---|---|---|---|
| We all feel that we're important to the work group. | | | | People feel that they are taken for granted. |

5.  How often is recognition given for good performance?

| 1 | 2 | 3 | 4 | 5 |
|---|---|---|---|---|
| Appreciation for a good job is expressed; anger is not. | | | | Good performance goes unnoticed, but mistakes do not. |

*Behaviors*                                    *Consequences*

## INVOLVEMENT

6.  To what degree do people feel they are a real part of what happens?

| 1 | 2 | 3 | 4 | 5 |
|---|---|---|---|---|
| We all feel at home all the time. | | | | Some people always feel left out. |

7.  To what degree do people feel they have influence with the boss?

| 1 | 2 | 3 | 4 | 5 |
|---|---|---|---|---|
| New ideas are encouraged and judged on their merits. | | | | New ideas are neither encouraged nor noted. |

*Behaviors*                                        *Consequences*

## COMMITMENT TO PERFORMANCE

8.  How well does this unit work at its tasks?

| 1 | 2 | 3 | 4 | 5 |
|---|---|---|---|---|
| Works well, manages differences, achieves goals. | | | | Coasts, ignores or suppresses differences, makes no progress. |

9.  What is the level of responsibility for work?

| 1 | 2 | 3 | 4 | 5 |
|---|---|---|---|---|
| We each assume personal responsibility for the work. | | | | No one but the boss assumes responsibility for the work. |

*Behaviors*                                        *Consequences*

# CHAPTER 7
# MANAGING DIFFERENCES
# AND HANDLING CONFLICTS

Differences and conflicts seem to abound in everyday business life. In fact, working through differences and resolving conflicts are very much a part of a manager's job. Perhaps a manager experiences the most uncomfortable moments when handling differences and conflicts between people. Frequently, such situations create disagreements or arguments that the manager may be unprepared to deal with adequately.

Many people have been taught that differences in interpersonal situations are undesirable. Some management training programs in industry have even been designed to teach participants why it is necessary to avoid conflict and how to suppress it, should it occur. In this context, differences and conflict are used interchangeably to describe the same thing.

However, differences and conflicts will be used here to classify separate stages in a given situation. It will be assumed that differences are inevitable in human relationships. Far from being abnormal or undesirable, they can serve a valuable purpose in any organization if they are managed well. Conflict, on the other hand, is characteristic of situations where two or more parties are unable to see common solutions to their interdependent needs. Zero sum conditions where one party *must* lose is what characterizes a conflict situation.

Differences are neither intrinsically bad nor good. They do not necessarily contribute to either productive growth or destructive stagnation. Whether differences are functional depends, instead, on how they are handled and what results from this action. Consequently, managers must learn how to manage differences and use them to the best of their ability. If a manager can learn to manage differences well, the number of conflicts to be handled will be reduced. Let's look first at how to manage differences and then review some techniques for handling conflict.

## DIFFERENCES — OPPORTUNITIES FOR IMPROVEMENT

People in an organization may agree on an intellectual level that everyone makes a necessary and important contribution to fulfilling organizational goals. But on an emotional level they are likely to believe that their own problems are the most important and the allocation of scarce resources to their projects the most necessary. In many organizations, for example, operations tends to blame maintenance for equipment breakdowns, while maintenance blames operations for not taking care of the machinery. In this same vein, marketing units tend to criticize manufacturing units for being too slow and too conservative, while manufacturing tends to look on marketing as not being cost conscious or dependable. Consequently, each accuses the other of not looking at the situation from an overall company point of view.

The problem-solving orientations and long-range accountabilities of various units in an organization create these differences. The differences that are apparent between individuals and units in many organizations are simply a by-product of the specialization that has been developed and rewarded over time. It is natural that salesmen should value company responsiveness to customers, while operations managers should desire long production runs and planned changes. It is expected that staff people want to make changes while line personnel want things to remain as they are.

Ross Webber, of Wharton's School of Finance and Commerce, is an avid proponent of encouraging managers to be proactive in working through various interdepartmental differences.[1] In addition, he believes that the dilemmas that underlie many interdepartmental differences involve either one or some combination of the following factors:

- Flexibility versus stability;
- Short- versus long-term performance criteria;
- Quantitative versus qualitative results.

Interdepartmental differences can create or sustain the more commonly described "personality conflicts" that exist between individuals in two separate departments. Although differences in personality and compatibility do exist, more often than not such an element is only a peripheral factor in disputes.

Sometimes it is supposed that personality conflicts are the underlying cause of differences between people or units in an organization. Consequently, these people may be urged to sit down together and simply talk through their differences. However, most of the differences between people in organizations are caused not by incompatible personalities but by *incompatible accountabilities*. Disagreements may be aggravated by opposite personalities, but they are seldom caused by them.

Thus, managers must be skilled in working through what are probably work-related differences manifested and sealed by interpersonal dissension. These differences may arise in their own work groups or between employees who report to them and employees who report to other managers in the organization. In most cases, apparent personality conflicts are a reflection of something deeper and more basic than divergent views; they usually relate to the way work is done in the entire organization.

## UNDERSTANDING DIFFERENCES

People are not likely to reach an adequate compromise for a difference between them unless they clearly work through the nature and the reasons for their disagreement. Robert Tannenbaum and Warren Schmidt, professors at UCLA's Graduate School of Management, suggest that differences can best be understood by assessing whether the disagreement is over (1) facts, (2) goals, (3) methods, or (4) values. If people who disagree with each other can view their differences in terms of one of these categories, it will be easier for them to focus their attention on resolving the problem.[2] Such effort usually results in more discussion and less blaming than does an approach that avoids analyzing the nature of a difference. Where to begin in managing differences certainly affects how they end.

Sometimes a disagreement occurs because individuals have different definitions of the problem, are aware of variant pieces of relevant information, accept or reject divergent information as factual, or have differing impressions of their respective power and authority. These are all differences over facts.

Occasionally the disagreement is about what should be accomplished—i.e., which objectives of the department, division, section, or project are desirable. Differences over goals result from divergent views of the ideal situation.

Individuals also differ about the procedures, strategies, or tactics that would most likely achieve a mutually desired goal. These differences over methods include deciding on the best, the most efficient, and the most economical route to follow.

Disagreements over values are also common. Determining the way power should be exercised, what constitutes justice and fairness, and what is best for the organization in the long run is not always unanimous. These differences in priorities may, in turn, affect the choice of either goals or methods.

Arguments are prolonged and confusion is increased when the contending parties are not clear on the nature of the disagreement. By determining the source of the dispute, a manager will be in a better position to determine how to utilize and direct the disagreement for both the short- and the long-term good of the organization.

## A PROCESS TO BE MANAGED

The cost of unmanaged conflicts can be very high, but the gains from using differences effectively can also be very great. When differences are effectively managed, they help people clarify their perspectives and cause appropriate aspects of an issue to surface.

Sometimes people in a unit believe in and live by an unspoken policy that there should be no differences. So they give in or compromise or just remain silent when a situation arises that could spark differences. A modern parable created by management consultant Jerry Harvey illustrates how superficial agreement can adversely affect the decisions we make.[3]

### The trip to Abilene

A young man and his bride are visiting her folks in the small town of Coleman, Texas, which is in a dry, wind-blown section of the state. It is the middle of summer and there is not much to do, but the young couple and the in-laws are making the best of difficult climatic conditions by drinking lemonade and playing dominoes. All in all, the family is having a pretty good time, when suddenly the father-in-law says, "Why don't we drive to Abilene and have dinner in the cafeteria?" The young man thinks to himself, "Go to Abilene in this dust storm and heat? And in a car that isn't air-conditioned? There's nothing I want to do *less* than drive to Abilene." Abilene is fifty-three miles from Coleman, over a winding, dusty road. The young husband knows that, in order to keep the wind from blowing the dust into the car, they will have to drive with the windows up. He also knows that the only place to eat that is open on Sunday afternoon offers food that leaves much to be desired.

But the young wife says, "Sounds like a great idea, don't you think, honey?" So, in order to please her, he replies, "Sure, I'm game if everyone else is willing. How do you think your mother will feel about it though?" The mother-in-law is asked, and she says she wants to go, so all four pack into the family car and make the hot, dusty trip to Abilene. When they arrive there, they eat the predictably unpleasant meal, crowd back into the car, and drive fifty-three miles home.

Finally, worn-out, hot, tired, dusty, irritable, they arrive back at the house and find another glass of lemonade. One by one, each expresses relief that the ordeal is over. Then, startlingly, they discover that no one really wanted to go to Abilene. Each simply went along with the idea, believing that the others were interested in the trip. None of the four voiced any reservations because no one wanted to "spoil it" for the others. They simply wanted to be agreeable.

In organizations, people take symbolic trips to Abilene when they fail to express their deep-seated concerns or when they attempt to suppress differences rather than deal with them. When it comes to searching for alternative courses of action for various problems, the differences among employees in every organization can help to increase the range and variety of viable choices.

Channeling differences into a problem-solving context may also help deal with some of the feelings that often accompany disagreement—frustration, resentment, and hostility. By providing an open and accepting approach, the manager helps prevent the development of undercurrents of feelings that could break out at inopportune moments. The open approach also helps channel the energy these feelings generate into creative rather than destructive activities. Destructive conflict tends to cause individuals to seek ways of weakening and undermining those who differ with them, but a problem-solving approach leads individuals to welcome differences as being potentially enriching to personal goals, ideas, and methods.

## STRATEGIC CONSIDERATIONS

A manager should determine to what extent disagreement is due to facts, goals, methods, and values, respectively. Differences over facts are usually easier to manage than differences over values, although each can be handled through conscious effort. When differences seem to arise from divergent perceptions of the facts in a situation, a manager should ask "What has produced the result of two people viewing the same information in different ways?" In this way, a manager begins to look for factors that might have caused the separate views of the situation.

Differences over methods occur most frequently and are perhaps the easiest to handle. When a disagreement over methods arises, a manager may want to note that there is apparent agreement over ends rather than over means. Then, building on this agreement, the establishment of an independent set of criteria for evaluating alternative means can be suggested. In addition, the manager should ask "What can I do to help these people see my role as I see it?"

If the differences are over goals or priorities, it can be useful to clarify the desired outcomes. In particular, by describing objectives in operational terms various issues can be discussed more realistically. Sometimes differences persist simply because what each party wants is not sufficiently clear.

Differences over values can also be dealt with better if desired outcomes can be put in operational terms. In such cases, it is easier to identify and test assumptions and to examine the possibility of various consequences actually occurring. Since value-related issues usually flow from past experiences and not just from current thinking, it is important to include both facts and feelings as appropriate data for discussion.

Some of the time, our values are the result of significant emotional events that made a deep impression. Thus, one person may not want to live in Columbus, Ohio, because of once running out of gas there while making a cross-country trip and having to walk some distance to the nearest gas station. This person could probably not be convinced to relocate to Columbus on the basis of the city's desirable cost of living, recreational facilities, and the like. Facts did not produce the value orientation and facts will not change it. Recognizing the basis of our value orientations, however, can help us to examine them and determine whether they are valid.

### Win-win and win-lose orientations

Organizations depend on the proper management of differences if they are to function effectively. When one part fails to mesh

STRATEGIC CONSIDERATIONS    111

with other parts, the whole organization is jeopardized. Failure of any unit can threaten the whole company.

Consultants Robert Blake, Herb Shepard, and Jane Mouton maintain that there are five positions available for each party in a disagreement.[4] Diagrammatically, these five positions can be explained in terms of two dimensions: personal concern for influencing the decision and personal concern for maintaining a positive relationship (see diagram on next page).

In position 1, differences are ignored and avoided. Position 2 describes situations like the Abilene parable already mentioned. The premium is placed on harmony and getting along. Position 3 is a win-lose orientation, a situation in which the unit is willing and able to forego any long-term objective in order to gain a short-run tactical advantage. Position 4 is marked by bargaining, trading, or compromising. The emphasis here is on splitting the difference, with each party giving a little. Position 5 is genuine problem solving. Here the effort is *not* devoted to determining who is "right" or "wrong", and it is *not* devoted to yielding something in order to get something in return. Instead, it *is* devoted to a genuine effort to search for alternatives that are mutually acceptable.

### "How to" techniques

Some things help two or more people, groups, or districts use differences to solve problems. Some things inhibit them from engaging in this. Here are some actions and attitudes for you to consider for getting into a problem-solving mode and for helping you come up with creative solutions to differences.

1. *Get in touch with your own emotions.* It is often difficult to retain objectivity while trying to work through differences. However, unless you are aware of your own emotional involvement, you will be unable to manage differences well. One way to get in touch with these emotions is to ask yourself "What is going on right here and now?" This question can help you take a step back and examine the situation. In addition, giving a response that is emotionally bland can also contribute to tension reduction. A well-timed "oh," "I see," or "mmm" can accomplish that purpose.

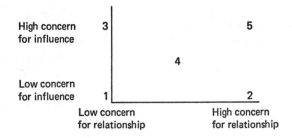

2. *Acknowledge the feelings of others.* Sometimes a manager can do things that inhibit working through differences. Instead of denying the feelings of others with generalizations such as "Everyone has problems like that," a manager should communicate respect for other points of view. Active listening statements such as "I see why you feel that way" or "Sounds like you're upset about this" can convey such respect.

3. *Intellectualize the concern.* When differences are put in a problem-solving mode, they are easier to manage. One way to do this is to express concerns or disagreements in an action-oriented, "how to" form. For instance, replacing such statements as "Are you kidding? Top management would never buy that!" with "How would you make that proposal acceptable to top management?" can help. Putting differences in writing so that they can be more easily analyzed can also help.

4. *Explore options.* Too often differences persist because the search for mutually acceptable options is brief and incomplete. You should frequently ask such questions as "What would happen if . . . ?" and "What might we be overlooking?"

5. *Make summaries and check for consensus.* This is important to do regularly when working through differences. It provides direction to a conversation and tends to ensure that both parties reach an agreement at approximately the same time. In this regard a phrase like "What each of us will do, then, is . . ." can be very helpful.

## CONFLICTS—A DIFFERENT PROBLEM

Handling conflict is not the same as managing differences. In conflict, people or organizations have joint but inevitably contrary interests. In such adversarial relations as typically exist between management and unions, buyers and sellers, and regulators and regulatees, conflict should be expected and appropriately planned for.

People in conflict situations often express their goals and aspirations in ambiguous terms, such as the following:

- "I just want to do what's best for everyone."
- "I just want to get what I am due."
- "I want to get over this hurdle so that we can move on to something else."
- "I want to make sure that we do the right thing."

Each of these statements express undertones of rightness or fairness. They represent feelings of wanting to see justice done. The basic incompatibility of interests creates conflict and makes conflict situations distinct from relatively simple differences. Consequently, a manager must be prepared to handle conflict with an approach different from the one used to manage differences. Otherwise, the goals will not be achieved.

## UNDERSTANDING CONFLICT

Conflict, like differences, is neither good nor bad. It can produce beneficial results, as illustrated by the separation of powers in the federal government, or it can produce disaster. Specific actions that escalate destructive conflict can be identified, and a manager should avoid them. One of the more pervasive conflict escalating actions is a heavy reliance on overt manipulation and covert threats. If one person feels another is becoming less reasonable, the first person may resort to subtle threats in order to make the important points. Unfortunately, this action usually shifts attention away from the issues being discussed and becomes a struggle to see who can belittle whom the most.

Another action that escalates conflict is placing emphasis on who is right and what is fair. Naturally, both parties believe they are right and most fair or there would be no conflict. Consequently, emphasizing this position serves very little purpose. Moreover, it tends to create an "Oh, yeah? Well, I'll show you" attitude that burns bridges instead of building them.

A final action that adds fuel to a conflict situation is failing to listen. In order to arrive at some kind of settlement, communication and understanding are required. When someone stops listening, it is likely that the others will look on that person as unreasonable and impossible to work with rationally. Consequently, they will tend to see hostile methods as the only recourse open to them.

Just as there are specific actions that escalate conflict, so there are specific actions that can channel it into appropriate modes and make it productive. These actions may not turn a conflict situation into one of complete collaboration, but they can make it much more productive and beneficial. They can turn a disintegrating situation into a problem-solving one.

Many conflicts result in mutually beneficial outcomes to all parties involved when at least one or each person involved reexamines current positions in the light of new information. This implies being willing to accept new information and to consider a variety of alternatives. All too often people tend to quickly grab a position when conflict seems apparent. They may then simply defend this position, relishing the security that comes from being immovable and unshakeable. However, by continually searching for new options and being willing to consider new information, people can be set free to consider mutually beneficial courses of action.

Declaring intentions can also serve to channel conflict into a productive mode. As a result of such an action, others have a clear understanding of the manager's operating base as well as of the conditions all are working to achieve. This always allows the other party to block these intentions if they so desire. If they do this, however, a stalemate is more likely to result than is the fact that the manager was taken advantage of. Neither party gains and both lose in such a situation. But usually, by declaring intentions, a manager is extending a goodwill gesture that is generally reciprocated.

A third action that can make a conflict situation more productive is to be output-oriented: What can be learned from the fact that conflict exists? What does it say about the orientations of the conflicting parties? What does each *really* want (not just what they say they want)? Answers to these and other questions not only aid understanding but also focus energies into obtaining a product—an agreeable plan. Being output directed can greatly enhance conflict resolution.

## Negotiation techniques

Since conflict situations involve the existence of two or more people or groups who possess basically divergent needs and goals, a manager must be skilled in a variety of negotiation techniques in order to profit from such situations. Let's examine several versatile techniques and see how they might be used.

One important technique is to "aim high" in negotiating and to continue to work toward this high aspiration level. In negotiations, as in life, it appears that those with high aspirations do better than their counterparts. This was amply illustrated in an experiment conducted by Larry Fouraker, Dean of the Harvard Business School. Fouraker built a barricade between various sets of bargainers so that neither could see or hear the other. Demands, offers, and counter-offers were to be passed under a table. The instructions given to each bargainer were identical except that one person in each set was told to achieve a settlement above $7.50, while the other person in the bargaining set was instructed to settle for $2.50. The experiment was designed to favor neither party. Each bargainer had an equal chance of settling for $5.00, if desired. The interesting result of the experiment was that those who were told to get $7.50 obtained that sum, while those who were told to get $2.50 got $2.50. What each expected, each obtained.[5]

Aspiration level, risk-taking, and successful negotiation are related. People who set higher targets regarding expected outcomes in a negotiation do better than those willing to settle for less. What people really expect, they work to achieve. Consequently, a manager should decide what results from a negotiation session are really wanted, write down these desirable outcomes, and then use them as guides in each negotiation.

Another important skill effective negotiators have learned relates to their use of personal power. Power is interpersonal, dependent on such factors as:

- each person's perception of mutual interdependence;
- the other's perception of *your* resources, real or imagined, that can help realize the other's goals;
- each person's status.

How each person in a conflict situation views the other along these dimensions will affect results. Often, managers will underestimate their own power or overestimate that of another.

Power is a quality that depends greatly on the abilities of a manager and on the perceptions it can create in the minds of others while negotiating. Chester Karrass, author of *The Negotiating Game*, has described four ways in which power can be understood and used effectively.[6]

1. One person may be in a preferred position relative to the other, but if neither one of them recognizes the advantage, there is none.

2. The fact that one position is more supportable by logic or evidence does not guarantee success. Also, if the consequences that person A can impose on person B are considered unimportant by B, then A will have no power over B.

3. Power may be exercised without action. If someone believes that some consequence can or will be imposed on him, it may be unnecessary to actually use it.

4. The ends of power cannot be separated from the means. In exercising power, exploitive means produce short-lived victories. A continuing relationship requires means that compliment the desired ends.

Negotiating is not a contest to see who can win. It is not necessary for one person or party to emerge "victorious" from a conflict situation. In fact, in most win-lose situations there are no winners, just losers. With a little effort, a better deal can be found for both parties at the same time. However, it is necessary for someone to channel the energies of each party into productive paths. The negotiation techniques that have been described can help a manager do just that.

## SUMMARY

"Two heads are better than one" because the two heads represent a richer set of experiences and because they can bring to a problem a wider variety of insights. For example, had the six blind men who touched different parts of the same elephant pooled their information, they would have come up with a more accurate description of the animal than any single one could give on the basis of his limited experience. In the same way, many problems can be seen clearly, wholly, and in perspective only if the individuals who see various aspects can pool their information.

At times, a manager will find situations where either differences or conflicts are apparent. No doubt there will be times when the manager is a contributing party, just as there will be other times when it will be necessary for the manager to act as a mediator. It may be difficult to deal with the emotions and feelings that are an inevitable part of such circumstances, but to dismiss those emotions as "unbusinesslike" or "inappropriate" is a mistake. Likewise, to deal with them in a haphazard or careless manner will only be sowing eventual ill-will.

There are systematic ways of dealing with differences and conflicts that can turn them into useful events. Approaching them with less apprehension and with a greater awareness of what can be done to turn them to advantage will aid the manager in discovering and implementing realistic alternatives to such situations. This may not be easy to do, but the rewards are worth the effort. When it comes to searching for alternative courses of action for dealing with a given problem, the differences among the individuals in an organization can help increase the range and variety of options.

## REFERENCES

1.  Ross H. Webber, *Management: Basic Elements of Managing Organizations.* Homewood, Ill.: Richard D. Irwin, 1975.

2.  Warren H. Schmidt and Robert Tannenbaum, "The Management of Differences," *Harvard Business Review,* November–December, 1960, pp. 107–115.

3.  Jerry B. Harvey, "The Abilene Paradox," *Organization Dynamics,* Summer, 1974, pp. 63–80.

4.  Robert R. Blake, Herbert A. Shepard, and Jane S. Mouton, *Managing Intergroup Conflict in Industry.* Houston: Gulf Publishing, 1964.

5.  Sidney Siegal and Lawrence E. Fouraker, *Bargaining and Group Decision-Making.* New York: McGraw-Hill, 1960.

6.  Chester L. Karrass, *The Negotiating Game.* New York: Thomas Y. Crowell, 1970.

# PART III
# THE DECISIONAL
# FUNCTION

# CHAPTER 8
# HOW TO MAKE
# A GOOD DECISION

There is nothing in the world that is so common and yet so difficult to make as a tough decision. Every day managers are confronted with choices and situations that demand decisions. All managers are decision makers, and their effectiveness as managers is largely reflected in their "track record" in making the "right decision". Experience in making decisions, however, does not ensure that they will necessarily be easier or better. Decision making, unlike some other skills, may not improve with repetition. Moreover, many decisions are not easy to make, and simply weighing the pros and cons involved is seldom enough to accurately decide the best course of action to pursue. President Warren G. Harding expressed the dilemma other decision makers have undoubtedly faced when he confided to a friend:

John, I can't make a damn thing out of this tax problem. I listen to one side and they seem right, and then I talk to the other side and they seem just as right, and there I am where I started. I know somewhere there is a book that would give me the truth, but hell, I couldn't read the book. I know somewhere there is an economist that knows the truth, but I don't know where to find him and haven't the sense to know him and trust him if I did find him. What a job![1]

Whatever their causes, the problems involved in decision making are often magnified because managers do not have a framework to use when making a decision. It is not enough for a manager to get all of the facts and evaluate alternatives before making a decision. Knowing which facts to get and how to evaluate the alternatives is equally important. Although there are no simple ABC's for decision making, there are some guidelines that can make the process smoother and the results better. These include:

- knowing when and when not to decide;
- setting explicit objectives or having desired outcomes in mind before gathering information;
- taking the best from each alternative, not just the best alternative;
- taking action that gets results; and
- following through in a manner that builds employee commitment.

## DECIDING TO DECIDE

An important first step in the decision-making process is simply deciding to decide. Managers should regularly ask themselves such questions as "Is this something I should decide, or does someone else have better information?" and "Should I act alone, consult with others, or get everyone together to decide on this one?" How such questions are answered is important. One of the main tasks of a manager is to build and maintain a set of criteria for deciding who should be involved in making a particular decision.

In many situations, the complexities involved in a particular matter require the coordination and honest inputs of many different people. Generally a manager cannot know or control enough of the operations of the unit to make all decisions alone. Thus, knowing when and how to involve others who are appropriate becomes extremely important.

One way to think about decision making is to view an effective decision as a product of both the quality or rationality of the decision and the commitment of people to implement it.[2] Thus, quality or rationality depend on such factors as getting accurate information, evaluating alternatives, and exercising judgment. Commitment or acceptance, however, depend on such things as involving key people in the decision process and identifying the advantages of a course of action to the people who are affected by it. In some situations, the quality of a decision may be the most important factor to consider, such as in whether to expand a product line or go into a new market. The effectiveness of such decisions depends to a great extent on getting information that is probably limited to just a few people in the organization. In these situations, a manager may want to get information from subordinates and make the decision alone or join a few subordinates and make the decision with them. In other situations, commitment may be the most important factor to consider, as in the case of who will be required to work overtime on an undesirable project or how to get the supervisors to accept the company's affirmative action plan. Where commitment is important, a manager should invite all who will be affected by the decision to a group meeting where their ideas can be shared and their acceptance secured.

Deciding who will decide, then, is an important first step in the decision-making process. Depending on the relative importance of quality and commitment, managers should select an approach to be taken. It is important to realize as well that the decision of who will decide will probably have a significant impact on the eventual outcome of the course of action chosen.

## Setting objectives

A frequent error committed by managers in decision making is the tendency to skip over setting objectives to evaluating alternatives. This is a mistake. Setting objectives focuses a manager's attention on where he must go to get the information needed to accurately assess the implications of a problem. Without objective setting, the search for information will be more costly and much less efficient than it could otherwise be.

By starting with the results that are expected to be achieved a manager can better decide what information is needed. This is no mean accomplishment. It is often very difficult to develop a clear picture of a problem or opportunity, phrased in operational terms, but it is important to do so. Peter Drucker, a well-known management consultant, emphasizes this point by often contrasting decision making in the United States with decision making in Japan:

> In the West, all the emphasis is on the *answer* to the question. Indeed, our books on decision-making try to develop systematic approaches to giving an answer. To the Japanese, however, the important element in decision-making is *defining the question*. . . . Japanese managers may come up with the wrong answer to the problem, but they rarely come up with the right answer to the wrong problem.[3]

In order to get a clear picture of the results wanted, a manager might ask some of the following questions:

- What needs to be accomplished?
- Where are there problems currently?
- How will everyone know when things have improved?
- What returns on invested time as well as money are expected?
- What unintended consequences are possible? How could they be minimized?
- What resources are available?

The answers to these questions will keep a manager results-oriented and will provide a focus for the decisions to be made.

## Getting information

The most expensive aspect of decision making tends to be the time spent gathering the information necessary for generating and analyzing alternatives. It is one thing to say "Get all of the facts" and quite another to actually do it. Moreover, what may be a fact to one person is merely an opinion to another. For in the reality of business operations, "facts" are dependent on a criteria of relevance. The fact that the scrap rate is 6% or that the market share for a product is 15% means nothing unless someone decides that the figures are too high or too low. Thus, a part of getting worthwhile, usable information is determining criteria that are useful indicators.

It is not easy to get the necessary information that a decision usually requires. Some people even misuse the information gathering phase of decision making. They go on and on getting advice, doing research, and assembling data and never reach any conclusions. When a manager starts wanting more and more information without coming to any conclusions, her ways should be reconsidered. In management, there are no fail-safe solutions, no options that will ensure a perfect decision. After all, if judgment wasn't necessary in the managerial process there would be no need for the manager.

The amount of information needed for a decision is probably best thought of as a function of the decision's magnitude. Those decisions that are difficult to reverse or expensive to change should be studied as thoroughly as possible. Those decisions that are not expensive to change should be made quickly. Robert Townsend, a former board chairman, illustrates the distinction between these two kinds of decisions:

> A decision to build the Edsel or Mustang (or locate your new factory in Orlando or Yakima) shouldn't be made hastily, nor without plenty of inputs from operating people and specialists.

> But the common or garden-variety decision—like when to have the cafeteria open for lunch or what brand of pencil to buy—should be made fast. No point in taking three weeks to make a decision that can be made in three seconds—and corrected inexpensively later if wrong.[4]

Perhaps the most important aspect of this information-getting function is the search for data, not merely for opinions. People have a tendency to accept someone else's evaluation of a situation without probing for that person's reasons for the conclusion. There is nothing wrong with opinions, but they should be supportable. Thus, a manager can test the information those who report to him have supplied by asking such questions as:

- How do I know this is accurate?
- Is there operational data to support these conclusions? That is, would an outsider have to ask what is meant by "too high," "not enough," etc.?
- Will this information help evaluate alternative courses of action?

Having good information is a necessary prerequisite to the accurate evaluation of available alternatives.

### Evaluating alternatives

The results-oriented manager understandably assumes that in most situations there are things that need to be done to improve the organization's overall effectiveness. This desire to act pushes many managers into poor decisions that could be avoided if time were spent carefully listing and considering available options. Although it is time-consuming, it is necessary. The Bay of Pigs fiasco in the early days of the Kennedy administration is just one example of what can happen when alternatives are not carefully explored before a decision is made.

Alfred P. Sloan Jr., former chairman of the board of General Motors, apparently believed in the importance of looking at all alternatives and exploring the potential of each before making any significant decision. Sloan is reported to have said at one GM executive committee meeting, "Gentlemen, I take it that we are all in complete agreement on the decision here." After everyone around the table nodded in assent, he continued, saying, "Then I propose we postpone further discussion of this matter until our next meeting to give ourselves time to develop disagreement and perhaps gain some understanding of what the decision is all about." Sloan recognized that there is always at least one valid reason for *not* pursuing a particular course of action. If they have not surfaced and been analyzed, it is a sign that alternatives have not been adequately explored. Sloan was not interested in making "decisions by oversight," so he requested that the group reconvene at a later date to discuss the matter further.[5]

Of course, the effectiveness of generating and evaluating alternatives depends on a realistic search for options. Sometimes poor decisions are made because of a manager's preconceptions about what will work and what will not. Getting others together in a meeting can help a manager avoid this trap, since others can often be relied on to bring fresh perspectives and different opinions.

The proper utilization of such an approach depends, however, on the creation of a group climate where each person feels free to express individual ideas. One way to develop such a climate is to avoid the common assumption that there is only "one right way to go." Those who believe that only one course of action can be right and that all others must therefore be wrong inhibit the evaluation of alternatives. Instead, the focus should be kept on more workable versus less workable alternatives.

The value of generating a list of possible alternatives when confronted with a decision that must be made and then selecting the best option is almost universally recognized as a basic part of decision making. Unfortunately, that is usually where the advice stops. How a manager goes about developing and evaluating alternatives is generally neglected. One technique for this process is brainstorming.

Brainstorming is a conscious attempt to promote alternative generation by separating it from evaluation. Frequently, managers evaluate alternatives as they develop them and cease their search when a satisfactory choice is formed. Brainstorming attempts to alter this habit by requiring that a specific amount of time be allocated to simply listing alternatives. After the search has been exhausted, each alternative can be evaluated by writing down its advantages and disadvantages (concerns to be reckoned with appropriately, as described in the next chapter).

There is a simple technique for evaluating alternatives. For each alternative, identify the worst thing that could possibly happen if implemented. This can be done by writing a scenario depicting all possible negative consequences that might occur. Then list those things that are most likely to result and the reasons why such outcomes could be expected. If applied faithfully, this method of analysis tends to assure that options are evaluated for their workable content.

## Taking action

The value of any decision can be measured by the positive impact it has on the people and things it affects. For some decisions, it is not necessary to obtain employee commitment to its implementation in order for it to have its intended impact. For other decisions, however, commitment is vital. In one large company, for instance, the manager of the computer operations decided to purchase a new computer that would allow the unit to run its programs much more quickly and efficiently. The manager told no one of the decision and had the equipment installed during a three-day weekend. When the employees returned to work, they discovered that they would be required to learn some new procedures for processing work in order to use the new equipment. After several weeks, however, the new equipment had to be taken out and replaced with the old computers. The employees were so disgruntled with the way the change was made that performance had steadily dropped and literature on organizing a white-collar union had suddenly appeared.

How a manager takes action—the way decisions are implemented—is not something that can be left unanalyzed. Deciding how to implement decisions that will need the commitment of all key people must be done before taking action. Getting these key people involved in either defining the problem or in actually deciding how to go about implementing the decision are both useful ways to obtain commitment. When people are involved and informed, it is easier to obtain their commitment, as the old saying maintains: "What I am not up on, I may be down on."

No decision should actually be made by managers until action steps are spelled out. Until then, they have only good intentions. Converting such intentions into action, moreover, necessitates their answering such questions as:

- Who should know of this decision before implementation?
- What specific action steps will make implementation possible?
- Who should do what?
- How can responsibility be communicated and affixed?

The first and last of these questions are often overlooked. However, getting key people involved early is one way a manager communicates to them respect. It says, in essence, "I think enough of you to want your views and ideas on this matter." In addition, the last of these four questions, about communicating and affixing responsibility, is the key to getting motivated behavior. When a manager makes a decision that requires people to change their procedures on work they are currently doing, the best way to ensure that such changes will be made is to have people accept more responsibility. What people are responsible for, they do.

It is important, then, to consider what action commitments a specific decision requires, what work assignments follow from it, and who will be required to carry it out. Decisions rarely "make themselves;" action-oriented people must make them. But this still requires an organized effort to ensure that the decision is, indeed, implemented. Perhaps President Harry Truman was expressing some of his own frustration when he remarked, on the eve of his successor's inauguration, "Poor Ike. When he was a general, he gave an order and it was carried out. Now he is going to sit in that big office and he'll give an order and not a damn thing is going to happen." Truman knew the frustrations of trying to mobilize a large bureaucracy into action. He did, however, learn some effective ways to make things happen. One of these was the utilization of some basic techniques of delegation.

Delegation is an important key in implementing effective decisions. A manager cannot know enough or control enough to do everything alone, so others must often be depended on to implement any decisions. Delegation is one way to get key people involved and committed to a decision. When people are made to feel a part of a decision in this way, they naturally want to work hard to ensure that the decision is fully implemented.

## THE FOLLOW-THROUGH

When a decision has been made and action taken, a manager may consider that the decision-making job is done. However, the work is not going to get done as intended unless the manager has a consistent program for following through. This includes some time taken periodically to examine what has been done, assess outcomes to date, do some replanning, and review whether additional coaching or training is needed. Following through does not simply mean "checking up." Instead, it is establishing the times and methods for reviewing progress.

Many action plans that reflect the accumulation of sound decisions fail because of a lack of follow-up by the manager. A lack of follow-through may signal to employees that a manager has lost interest in a project or is no longer concerned about it. What people are rewarded for they tend to do. The attention and recognition that are by-products of following through is an important part of making a good decision.

Following through implies being willing to modify a course of action if such changes become necessary. This flexibility makes decision making easier since it removes some of the finality inherent in the decisions managers tend to make. As the novelist Somerset Maugham has written, "Half the difficulties of man lie in his desire to answer every question with a yes or no. Yes or no may neither of them be the answer; each side may have in it some yes or some no." Of course, some decisions must be made with a firm yes or no, but even then it is often possible to make a later modification. This is not being wishy-washy or indecisive. It is, instead, being open to new ideas and possible options as the fullest consequences of a decision are realized.

Being willing to go with a decision that is workable and open to modification as time passes can have a powerful freeing effect when one is faced with difficult choices. Lord O'Neill opened the clogged communication and decision-making channels in the British Parliament debate over Northern Ireland when he suggested that, instead of seeking a final solution, the conflicting parties try to arrive at a modus vivendi. "Instead of an ultimate solution to the matter," he suggested," why not consider an alternative that is agreeable which will automatically be reviewed within one year." His suggestion eventually led to the creation of the first provisional government in Northern Ireland.

## SUMMARY

In making genuinely big decisions, a manager must be prepared to stand a sense of loss as well as gain. Many decisions are not easily made or easily implemented. A part of being a manager is exercising judgment in difficult matters. Good decisions require both far-sighted judgment and a sense of timing, both of which are also important for knowing when not to make a decision. As Chester Barnard phrased it in his now-classic book *The Functions of the Executive,* "The fine art of executive decision consists in not deciding questions that are not now pertinent, in not deciding prematurely, in not making decisions that others should make."[6]

Premature decisions are perhaps the worst a manager can make. Too often it is too easy to rush into a situation and throw around judgments. Too often such haste, does indeed, make waste. Waiting can sometimes clarify the situation and bring the central issues into focus. Waiting and examining the intended and possibly unintended consequences of options can force a manager to look beyond the point at hand into the follow-through that a decision demands.

This is not indecision. On Monday morning quarterbacks are allowed the luxury of complete hindsight. Managers must act. They must often make choices on the basis of insufficient information or with inadequate consultation with others. If they are to capture opportunities and make things happen, managers must sometimes make decisions using only their intellect and their intuition.

Decision making is a rational process, but there are limits to its rationality. It is not a mechanical, lock-step procedure that can be easily taught or easily learned. Still, the processes that have been described, if consistently followed, can make any manager a better decision maker. Unfortunately, too many managers are inclined to cut these processes short in order to make a quick decision. Time sometimes helps and sometimes hinders effective decisions. How managers handle the time factor determines whether they make most decisions or whether most decisions are made for them. Conscious decision making, as opposed to crisis responding, separates the effective from the less-effective managers.

A final ingredient in the entire decision-making process has been reserved for last. It is difficult to describe adequately, perhaps impossible to practice completely. The final ingredient is commitment. Unpopular decisions are not easily made or implemented. It is not always possible to convince others that a particular course of action must be taken. But it is sometimes necessary to make decisions with which no one agrees. Such decisions seldom leave the decision maker exhilarated and confident. Still, the decisions must be made. For in business as in ordinary life, one person with courage and commitment is a majority.

## REFERENCES

1.  Cited in Andrew Sinclair, *Available Man: The Life Behind the Masks of Warren G. Harding.* New York: Quadrangle, 1969.

2.  For more on this idea, see Daniel Katz and Robert L. Kahn, *The Social Psychology of Organizations.* New York: John Wiley, 1966.

3.  Peter Drucker, *Management: Tasks, Practices, Responsibilities.* New York: Harper & Row, 1974, pp. 466–467.

4.  Robert Townsend, *Up the Organization.* New York: Alfred A. Knopf, 1970, p. 45.

5.  Cited in Peter Drucker, *The Effective Executive.* New York: Harper & Row, 1967.

6.  Chester Barnard, *The Functions of the Executive.* Cambridge: Harvard University Press, 1938, pp. 310–311.

# CHAPTER 9
# PROBLEM FINDING
# AND PROBLEM SOLVING

Managing effectively involves finding problems, coming up with creative solutions to them, and implementing these solutions in ways that make them work. How does a manager do these three things? Problems do not spring forth with identifying flags, and it is easier to say "come up with a creative solution to this problem" than to actually do it.

First of all, it is important to realize that a problem exists only when at least one person says it exists. The existence of a problem is a very subjective matter. However, a difference of any kind between what people say is happening and what they believe should happen is a problem. Whether it is a big problem depends on what the important decision makers feel the consequences of inaction will be. But at least it is possible to say that a problem is nothing more or less than something that one person says is a problem.

This definition is not included for semantic precision. It is, instead, included to emphasize the importance of a manager's seeking out and identifying acceptable standards of performance for both people and things so that problem finding and problem solving will be easier. Such standards of performance, or criteria of relevance, are the best guides for determining how well a manager is doing.

A manager's job, like that of a ship's captain, is to manage both people and equipment in such a way that a steady and predictable course is maintained and an intended destination eventually reached. These are not simple tasks. Moreover, they are extremely time consuming. Perhaps one of the greatest challenges of the modern manager is to get the necessary information concerning various problems in such a way that workable solutions to them can be generated. This is a challenge because the workload and demands placed on managers will force them into mediocrity if they do not take steps to consciously deal with superficiality and to actively manage their units. One way a manager can begin to do this is to spend time looking for problems that exist but have not yet been brought to attention.

## LOOKING FOR PROBLEMS

There are two main reasons why a manager should spend time periodically looking for problems: (1) to find out systematically what the overall strengths and weaknesses of that unit are; and (2) to discover new opportunities to improve the way work is currently being done. One way to begin such an activity would be to trace the progress of a single organizational output throughout the entire unit, looking for gaps between "what is" and "what should be."

In looking for differences between "what is" and "what should be," a manager can ask seven broad questions that will help locate possible gaps between expected and actual performance. These seven questions are:

1. Do employees see a purpose in each activity in which they are required to participate?
2. Is the work load distributed so that both division of authority and job enrichment are possible?
3. Do all necessary tasks have rewards and incentives for good performance?
4. Are available technologies and existing machinery being appropriately utilized?
5. How effective are existing methods for managing differences and handling conflicts?
6. What helps and what hinders current interactions with customers and suppliers?
7. How do I know that my answers to these questions reflect reality?

Answers to each of these questions can supply a manager with valuable information. But once the information is obtained, the manager must still decide how to *define* the problem. This is a most precarious task, because how the problem is defined will significantly affect the solutions to be eventually considered.

## DEFINING THE PROBLEM

There are a number of well-known situations that are excellent examples of how the definition of a problem affects the solutions considered. Perhaps two will suffice. One is the classic story of the truck that was stuck in an underpass. Various onlookers tried to be helpful by suggesting ways to free the truck. However, each suggestion involved considerable damage either to the truck or to the underpass. Then a little boy came along and suggested letting air out of the tires. Apparently, the little boy's perspective led to a definition of the problem different from the adults' and ultimately to a more acceptable solution.

Another well-known example is found in Mark Twain's book *Tom Sawyer*. At one point, Tom had been assigned to whitewash the picket fence that surrounded his aunt's house. There was no way to avoid the task. Tom, however, has a flash of inspiration when a neighbor boy happens along and the following dialogue ensues:

"Hello, old chap, you got to work, hey?"

"Why, it's you, Ben! I warn't noticing."

"Say—I'm going a-swimming, I am. Don't you wish you could? But of course you'd druther work—wouldn't you? Course you would."

Tom contemplated the boy a bit, and said:

"What do you call work?"

"Why, ain't that work?"

Tom resumed his whitewashing and answered carelessly:

"Well, maybe it is, and maybe it ain't. All I know, is, it suits Tom Sawyer."

"Oh come, now, you don't mean to let on that you like it?"

The brush continued to move.

"Like it? Well I don't see why I oughtn't to like it. Does a boy get a chance to whitewash a fence every day?"

That put the thing in a new light. Ben stopped nibbling his apple. Tom swept his brush daintily back and forth— stepped back to note the effect—added a touch here and there—criticized the effect again—Ben watching every move and getting more and more interested, more and more absorbed.

Presently he said:

"Say, Tom, let me whitewash a little."

Soon Tom has others joining in the task of whitewashing, even having them pay for the privilege. Tom succeeded in defining work as play, and his friends accepted this new definition of the situation.

These two examples illustrate the importance of defining a problem wisely and well. In doing so, it is vital to suspend judgment and try to get a clear picture of the nature of the problem before jumping to a conclusion. An experiment by the noted educator Jerome Bruner serves to illustrate this point. Bruner projected color slides of familiar objects on a large screen and asked people to try to identify them while they were still out of focus. He gradually improved the focus and called for reidentification at various times. His startling finding was this: If an individual wrongly identifies an object while it is still greatly out of focus, that person will generally be unable to correctly identify it when it is clearer. On the other hand, another person who has not seen the blurred image can easily identify it.[1] What this experiment seems to demonstrate is that more evidence is required to overcome an incorrect definition than is required to establish a correct one. A person who jumps to conclusions is less likely to see any other definition of a problem.

## REFRAMING PROBLEMS

One way to avoid jumping to conclusions and to define problems more accurately is to practice "reframing."[2] Reframing is trying to look for the obscure—trying to go beyond the apparent—in defining a problem. The term "reframing" is used because the person is attempting to change the frame of reference. Successful reframing does not include changing the facts but it does include changing the way the facts are viewed. Thus, Tom Sawyer did not change the facts of whitewashing the fence, but instead redefined work and thereby reframed the situation. Likewise, the little boy did not change the facts in the case of the truck in the underpass, but redefined the critical elements that needed changing to remedy the problem.

One company's employees demonstrated the practical significance of this technique on a tough problem they had. The problem involved the central activity of the business, transporting eggs from the farm to the grocery store. Egg breakage was excessive, and the company's employees were asked to come up with a solution that would reduce it. Several options were proposed, including training for the truck drivers, smoother-riding trucks, and sturdier egg cartons. Each proposal was expensive, however, and the benefits very uncertain. Then, someone in the group noted that each of the proposals assumed the problem was with the egg handlers. He then suggested that the problem be redefined as one of easily broken eggs, not of clumsy egg handlers. With the problem reframed in this way, a solution was proposed that included feeding the chickens something to make their egg shells more durable. A chemist in the group noted that this could be easily done. The company cut the egg losses in half when this solution was implemented.

Defining a problem is not a simple "once-and-for-all" step. Effectively defining a problem may mean carefully redefining it several times if it appears that particular definitions lead nowhere. However, it is important to conscientiously test each problem definition, both those that appear at first glance to be accurate and those that appear to lead nowhere.

### Retaining flexibility

Good problem solvers do not persist in defining a problem one way if that definition isn't leading anywhere. Instead, the good problem solver will jump from one definition of a problem to another until a workable solution is found. Poor problem solvers, on the other hand, doggedly maintain one and only one definition of a problem. A manager can learn to be a better problem solver, since that ability seems to be learned, not merely an inherent, unchangeable quality.

These conclusions have been validated by research performed by Norman R. F. Maier of the University of Michigan. One of Maier's experiments consisted of giving several hundred college students a battery of tests that required logical thinking and creative problem solving. With half of the students, Maier provided the problems with no preliminary comments. With the other half, he prefaced the test with a brief discussion of the following points:

1. Locate a difficulty and try to overcome it. If you fail, get it completely out of your mind and seek an entirely different difficulty.

2. Don't be a creature of habit. Don't stay in a rut. Keep your mind open for new ways to see the problem.

3. Solutions tend to appear suddenly. You cannot "will" them or force them. Keep your mind open for new relationships or new combinations and do not waste your time worrying about unsuccessful attempts at problem definition.

This brief lecture produced a significant improvement in the scores of the groups to which it was delivered. By encouraging the problem solvers to remain flexible and to redefine the problem when they were stumped, the students' problem-solving abilities were greatly enhanced.[3]

### Being problem-oriented

Although repeated attempts at defining a problem will not automatically ensure the development of a good solution, it will go a long way toward that end. In addition, remaining problem-oriented rather than solution-oriented will help in coming up with good solutions. One technique for doing this is the "positive response." This method is one way to respond to new ideas and to develop solutions that initially are not completely workable.[4]

Every idea or solution is born somewhere on a continuum between perfect and useless, as represented below:

It is like a baby, needing nourishment and protection. It may not be a perfect idea, but if it is not totally useless, how can it be developed? A positive response is one way to keep new ideas, like new babies, from being thrown out with the bath water.

A positive response consists of two parts. The first part is attempting to describe the positive, favorable characteristics of the new idea. The second part is describing any objections or concerns to the idea in a "how to" form. This is essentially what Teddy Roosevelt did when the idea of the Panama Canal was first proposed. Apparently, Roosevelt said something like, "The canal would provide a link between the east and west coasts. Militarily and economically, it would greatly help this country. But how to dig a canal in the mosquito-infested swamps and how to maintain a trained labor force to operate it are major concerns." When concerns are expressed in an operational manner such as this, they provide clues as to how the idea might be modified in order to become more acceptable. In this way, creative analysis results.

### Taking a break when stuck

Perhaps the most frequent advice given to people attempting to solve a tough problem is to take a break when stuck. But does it actually do any good?

Experiments at Stanford have demonstrated that taking a break can really help in problem solving as long as someone is truly stuck.[5] If, after exploring the possibilities of the present approach quite thoroughly, you cannot think of another approach to try, you are stuck. A break at this time will probably be helpful. However, if you are getting nowhere because the plan of attack does not quite seem to work or because the full dimensions of the problem are not fully understood, a break will probably not be helpful. Breaks can be useful for getting "untracked." But taking a break before actually feeling stuck will probably just lead back to the line of reasoning that was being considered before the break and will therefore not afford any significant benefit.

One technique for increasing the benefit of a break is to make use of a deliberately generated random stimulus. This technique, advocated by management consultant Edward de Bono, consists of selecting two numbers at random, the first to represent a page in the dictionary and the second to identify the position of a word on that page. The word that this random selection produces is then used to open up new avenues in thinking about the problem at hand.[6]

Suppose, for instance, an individual is concerned about the general problem of city traffic. Two random numbers, say 408 and 29, might lead to the word "pacemaker" in that person's dictionary. Trying to think of ways to combine "pacemaker" and the problem of city traffic is the next step. In a timed, four-minute period, here are some of the thoughts I came up with in applying this technique:

*pacemaker:* controls pace, regulates and maintains even flow, keeps traffic moving, prevents stops, prevents cars from getting on or off main streets at certain times of the day, except at designated locations, so that there are fewer stops and starts; paces cars with which traffic must keep up; determines different starting times for pacemaker or key industries in the city in order to stagger traffic.

These ideas are included to illustrate the practical significance of this idea. It is a powerful tool for generating new ideas and for changing directions when stuck.

### Talking it out

Another useful technique that can increase a manager's problem-solving effectiveness is to talk about the problem with someone else. In talking with someone openly about a problem, a person is forced to think more precisely. Taking short cuts or taking things for granted could spoil the anticipated results. Important fundamentals must be relied on in order to discuss the problem and its implications. This reality testing helps by forcing the manager to really know the subject.

In addition, the process of describing a problem and its implications may make a manager much more deliberate. This is because the problem is transformed from a private to a public forum. As noted by Jean Piaget, the distinguished Swiss psychologist and educator, logical thinking is improved when an individual is forced to justify plans or actions to another person.[7]

Somehow, talking things out helps a person see some of the unintended consequences of an action much more easily than would simply writing down the same words on paper. For whatever the reasons, it just seems that the give-and-take of a discussion crystalizes thoughts much better than does thinking things through alone.

Getting people together in a problem-solving conference can also help in the definition and analysis of problems. Norman Maier has concisely documented from research in business organizations the assets that are a part of group problem-solving efforts.[8] As found by Maier:

1. A group has more information than any one individual. One person may know more than any other group member, but the others will still have some additional relevant information.

2. Since individuals tend to have different perspectives on a problem, they are likely to push one another out of "ruts in thinking" when brought together as a group.

3. Groups tend to take more calculated risks than do individuals acting alone. If individuals know they do not have to "go it alone" in bearing responsibility for a solution's effectiveness, they are more likely to suggest and try out such solutions.

4. When the people who must carry out a decision are also involved in making the decision, their commitment to action is increased.

Group problem solving can be a valuable tool in the effective manager's hands, depending on how it is used. Just as there are clichés that condemn group problem solving ("a camel is a horse that has been put together by a committee"), so there are clichés that praise them ("two heads are better than one"). What every manager should do is neither wholly accept nor completely reject the wisdom of these two contradictory clichés. Instead, a manager should determine on a case-by-case basis whether group problem solving is appropriate.

## Planning for action

It is not always easy to forecast ahead of time what action steps are necessary to implement a problem's solution. One technique that can aid in planning for action is to consider how the solution will affect others in the organization. If it requires the support of higher level managers, how can a solution be packaged so that those people will support the proposed action and make it work?

Another technique that can help in planning for action is for a manager to ask "What could go wrong?" By asking and answering this question, emergency or contingency plans can be formulated. If Murphy's Law is to be believed ("If anything can go wrong, it will."), such forward thinking can avoid errors resulting from an incomplete analysis of a solution—i.e., taking it all the way through implementation. This kind of thinking is the basis for a technique known as "fault-free analysis," which is little more than allowing for implementation errors and making appropriate plans to deal with them beforehand. As common-sensible as this may seem, it is too often not common practice.

## SUMMARY

There are many conditions and events that can produce or create problems. Despite this diversity, the basic principles of problem finding and problem solving are few, simple, and general. Although problems can occur in a variety of contexts, it is possible to apply some consistent guides for more effective problem solving.

These guidelines do not dictate that the problem solver follow any lock-step, sequential steps in order to get good solutions to current concerns. Instead, these guidelines will provide managers with specific techniques that can be used to resolve problems more effectively. This material is intended to go beyond the common advice given to problem solvers, which is simply to locate the cause of a problem, get information on it, and do something about it. Although such advice may be good, it is not very useful. It amounts to little more than a suggestion to find the trouble and fix it.

The techniques that have been presented are rooted in solid research. They are also practical. Managers in a number of organizations have consistently applied many of them and found the results to be extremely beneficial. Of course, in order to work they must be used, and using them may be no small task. It takes more than good intentions to actually apply these problem-solving techniques. It also takes commitment.

When Warren Bennis was selected as the President of the University of Cincinnati, he acknowledged that he intended to implement a host of management principles. Unfortunately, he found that many of his innovations and intentions were way-laid by the sheer amount of administrative routines required of him as president of a large university. He found also that, unless he consciously made the effort to find problems and think through their implications as he attempted to resolve them, he would make superficial analyses and snap judgments. Many managers are faced with a similar situation. Unless a manager is committed to applying various problem-finding and problem-solving techniques, the workload will tend to force a more superficial analysis of pressing matters.

Managerial work is not easy. In order to be done well, it requires the manager to make things happen. Looking for problems and finding permanent solutions to them determine effectivness. Simply waiting for the problems and their solutions to appear will not work.

## REFERENCES

1. Jerome S. Bruner, *Beyond the Information Given: Studies in the Psychology of Knowing*. New York: Norton, 1973.

2. For more on reframing, see Paul Watzlawick, John H. Weakland and Richard Fisch, *Change: Principles of Problem Formation and Problem Resolution.* New York: Norton, 1974 and Eugene Raudseppand and George P. Hough, *Creative Growth Games.* New York: Harcourt Brace Jovanovich, 1977.

3. Norman R. F. Maier, *Problem-Solving Discussions and Conferences.* New York: McGraw-Hill, 1963.

4. For additional information, see *Managing for Innovative Teamwork.* Cambridge: Synectics, 1976.

5.  Cited in Ray Hyman and Barry Anderson, "Solving Problems," *Science and Technology*, September 1965, pp. 36–41.

6.  Edward de Bono, *Lateral Thinking for Management*. New York: Amacon, 1971.

7.  Jean Piaget, *The Psychology of Intelligence*. Boston: Routledge and Kegan Paul, 1971.

8.  Maier, *Problem-Solving Discussions*.

# CHAPTER 10
# TIME MANAGEMENT

Management, it has been said, is a series of interruptions interrupted by other interruptions. Managers perform a great number of tasks in a typical day, some of which are planned, while many others are not. However, finding enough time to do all the routine things that must be done in addition to putting out the daily "fires" that invariably start up can be both difficult and demanding. Managers can come to feel that they must work twice as fast in order to just stand still. They may come to feel that they will never be completely "on top of things."

Every manager must develop personal methods in order to meet the Niagara of demands that typify managerial work. Since most of a manager's day is unstructured, consisting of various blocks of discretionary time and an equal variety of discretionary tasks, matching tasks and time can be one of the more important decisions to make. Using time wisely and learning where to spend time profitably can make a difference in both individual and organizational performance. Wise time use can also give a manager a greater sense of purpose and a feeling of being in control of the work.

Most managers realize the importance of being in control of their work. Unfortunately, as soon as someone mentions setting priorities and budgeting time, the temptation is to get out paper, pencil, and ruler and make an elaborate chart allocating every minute of the day to some necessary function. Although such charts may be helpful, they can also be risky. They may hem a manager into performing duties that are of a lower priority than those that arise during the course of the day. Planning a day is useful if it allows for flexibility, but it is only one aspect of effective time management.

## FINDING TIME

Time is a unique resource. Everything takes time. The only real solution to handling time demands is to learn how to control events more and be controlled by them less. This process, however, does not begin with planning. Approaches to getting more done in less time that create detailed plans and allocate time among competing activities are probably doomed to the bottom of a desk drawer. Managerial work is simply not geared to such planning.

A different and more useful beginning point is for a manager to determine which tasks take up most of the work time. This beginning point is useful because it can help a manager see what things may need to be done differently in order to mange the time well. As Sune Carlson noted after a major study of Swedish managing directors, "It is quite a different thing for an executive to *feel* he does not have enough time to work alone or to discuss questions of development with his subordinates, and to *know* how much time he spent alone in his office during the last month, or how many times development questions actually were discussed during the same period."[1]

One technique for finding time is to keep a time inventory or time log. Peter Drucker emphasizes that this should be done by someone other than the manager in order to obtain an objective view of how time is spent.[2]

A secretary, for instance, could follow the manager around for a week, recording all activities in every 30-minute interval each day. The time log can help managers see where the time is *actually* spent, not simply where they *think* it is spent. This time analysis can help a manager decide what current duties could be done differently or not at all in order to find time for the things that really count.

## DISPOSING OF TIME WASTERS

Often, it seems, managers will tackle whatever tasks or opportunities are before them. Incoming mail just has to be opened, ringing telephones just have to be answered—or so a manager may think. However, consciously choosing the areas in which to invest effort is critical for effective time control. Some things are always less important than others; these should be identified and done only after the more important tasks have been performed. Managers can profit from the caution of the German poet Goethe, who once said, "Never let the things which matter most be at the mercy of things which matter least."

Common advice given to managers who want to improve their use of time is to "focus most on what contributes most" to the accomplishment of work objectives. The inverse of that statement, moreover, is also worthy. What does not contribute, but only wastes time? Try listing all the "time wasters" in a typical week or month and then rank order them according to the severity of time misuse they cause. Then ask such questions as these:

- What would happen if I didn't do this at all? Would it make a significant difference?
- Can I delegate this?
- Can I change this duty in order to make it more effective?

Listing and ranking wasteful uses of time can be an effective means of pinpointing activities that either someone else can do or need not be done at all. The primary criterion for evaluation should be: Does it make a difference?

Many time wasters stem from some aspect of an activity and not from the activity itself. Here are some activities that can easily slip from the productive time column to the wasted time column of a time balance sheet:

- *Telephone calls*. The frequency and length of calls can distract from more important matters.

- *Meetings*. Unplanned, mismanaged, or irrelevant meetings can make it more difficult for the next one to be good.

- *Visitors*. Unannounced, unscheduled people may have important business or they may just be looking for a little socializing.

- *Paperwork*. Some reports and memos should be read carefully and filed appropriately, while others should be discarded immediately.

- *Mail*. Reading publications and flyers may be interesting, but it can also be time-consuming.

Identifying the activities that waste time is the first step to reduce their effect or to eliminate them entirely. Time is like money. If it is spent wisely, it will bring good returns. If it is wasted, there will be nothing to show for the investment.

A manager should be careful in identifying and disposing of time wasters. Telephone calls, drop-in visitors, and other interruptions may require immediate attention; breakdowns in equipment or communication cannot be planned. However, a manager can and should develop a system for deciding what is really important and what is not.

## SETTING PRIORITIES

A manager can fall into a trap of being tyrannized by the urgent. In such cases, every project becomes a crisis and every order is a rush job. Subordinates learn that unless their work carries these labels it will probably be ignored, so they package it in the appropriate terms. Actually, only a few tasks are as urgent as some would make them out to be.

Setting priorities is one way to alleviate this situation or to make sure that you are heading in the right direction. After all, it is possible to become better and better at doing something that is not worth doing in the first place. One way to begin setting priorities is illustrated in the following incident.

> Several years ago a management consultant approached the president of a large steel corporation and outlined the firm's services. "No use," the president purportedly answered, "I'm not managing now as well as I know how. We need more doing, not more knowing. If you would get us to do what we know we should, I'll pay you anything you ask."
>
> "Fine," the consultant replied. "I can give you something in a few minutes that will greatly increase your doing what you know you should do. First, write on a blank piece of paper the five or six most important tasks that must be done tomorrow. Then prioritize them by putting them in order of their importance. Third, pull this sheet of paper out of your desk tomorrow morning and begin working on item one. When you finish item one, move on to number two, and so on until quitting time. Don't worry if you don't finish each item you had recorded or even if you only finished one item. You will at least be working on the most important things required of you. Lastly, take the last five minutes of each working day to make out a list of priorities for the following day."
>
> After six months, the president reportedly sent the consultant $25,000 for this idea—$1,000 for each of the twenty-five minutes spent in the visit.[3]

Listing priorities and budgeting time for their accomplishment is very important. Former UCLA management professor Joseph Trickett believes that important items and urgent items can be combined in setting priorities. Trickett suggests that work items be classified according to urgency on a scale ranging from "very urgent" to "not urgent" and then reclassified according to importance on a scale ranging from "very important" to "unimportant." Obviously, the highest priorities are assigned to those items that are both "very urgent" and "very important."[4]

Stress can be reduced by working on important matters that have pressing deadlines. When there is something really important to do, a manager should try to defer everything else until the next day. By postponing activities that can be postponed, a manager opens up a block of time to work on important matters.

## Segmentation

Every manager needs some time alone during the day to think and to do creative work. One of the most pervasive myths about time is that, since there is so little of it, each minute must be filled with some activity. Where such a belief prevails, it is possible for activity to be more highly regarded than productivity. In such situations, efficiency ("doing things in the right way") replaces effectiveness ("doing the right things"), and involvement supersedes completion. However, activity without achieving some kind of closure is pointless. Ultimately, what is actually accomplished is far more important than effort or sweat.

One way to get more things done is to carve out certain portions of the day and do only predetermined work during those periods. This idea of segmentation can also be extended to doing similar things all at once during the same time slot. Robert Townsend, formerly with Avis Rent-A-Car, applied this idea by telling the switchboard to connect calls for him only during 11–12 a.m. and 4–5 p.m. At other times, the switchboard people were to take the callers' names and numbers and indicate that he would call back. This technique allowed Townsend to group his calls and answer them all at once.[5]

Finding an uninterrupted hour to close the door and work on creative projects or pressing matters may be difficult, but it is very important. However, if carried to excess it can be counter-productive. It can cut a manager off from important people who need frequent access to the manager's ear. Watergate is perhaps testimony enough of the dire consequences that can occur when a manager decides to excuse himself from daily demands and to allow others too much control over who will and who will not be seen.

## Cultivating creativity

Time is something that everyone has in equal quantities. There are 24 hours in each person's day, 365 days in everyone's year. How a manager uses that time, then, either aids or limits overall effectiveness. If a manager's quiet time is limited, and every moment devoted to creative work must count, what can be done to make sure those equal moments are well spent? A few techniques that focus on creative powers can be practiced.

Creativity is elusive. It cannot be commanded, but it can be cultivated. Creativity cannot be willed, yet one can create *proper circumstances* in which creativity will more likely occur. Instead of demanding creativity, a manager must work in pleasant, conducive surroundings. This may vary depending on individual personalities. Churchill and Franklin Roosevelt, for instance, found midmorning hours in bed the most productive, while Wilson and Lincoln worked best late at night. Proper circumstances may mean a board room with no windows to draw a distracting gaze for one person and the smell of pine and a breathtaking view for another. Whatever the proper circumstances are, they need to be identified and consistently created.

A person further nurtures creativity by being surrounded by minds that are *sympathetic* to the objectives. This largely explains the success of most brainstorming sessions and sales meetings. Congenial associates with some common orientation and a common goal are able to reinforce each other, thereby increasing the proclivity to take risks and be inventive. This social support is requisite to the attainment of objectives.

Concentration is another means of encouraging creativity. Yet a manager who says "I must get this project completed by tomorrow. I'll just sit at my desk and put everything from my mind until it is done" is seldom successful. Invariably, the phone rings, or someone has a problem, or the pages of a report just stare back. Invariably, a person concentrates on the point of greatest interest, so *interest,* not concentration, must be manipulated.

Just as long-range objectives are less reinforcing and therefore more elusive than immediate goals, so are dispersed interests. Regardless of whether one is sitting at a wedding service, driving along a dangerous mountain road, or participating in a sales meeting, if something of greater interest comes along, such as news of a death or an accident, interest and concentration are immediately shifted to the new event.

If, then, the point of interest, not concentration, should be manipulated, how can interest in an object, action, or thought be conjured at will? The best method is close examination. Interest is motivated by close examination. Maybe that's why young lovers sit so closely together and spend hours looking at a curl, an eyelash, or a spot of dew on the lower lip. Moreover, interest motivates even closer examination, just as close examination motivates interest.

Creativity cannot be willed, yet circumstances favorable for eliciting it can be created. Being surrounded by minds that are sympathetic to the objectives also facilitates the ability to realize those objectives. Furthermore, concentrated power encourages creativity. Concentration also cannot be willed, but concentrating on the point of greatest interest can stimulate concentration. Finally, interest is generated and reciprocated by close examination.

## Delegation

Using techniques to be more creative can help a manager come up with better ideas. But what about implementing those ideas? And what about those projects passed up the line that others should be working on? Proper delegation can help in each of these circumstances. Cutting the workload down to only those things that are really important and then delegating the others can start effectiveness really soaring.

It is not uncommon to hear people who work with an over-loaded manager suggest delegation. Unfortunately, just turning the work over to someone else is not all there is to it. In fact, delegating more responsibilities will probably increase the demands on a manager's time initially. In the short run, delegation takes time because the manager must convey all known information about a task to the other person. Only over the long term will it free a manager for other things. Then delegation will give the manager more discretionary time because subordinates and others will be working on projects that really make a difference to the manager's own workload.

There are many reasons why a manager may not delegate even if it will eventually yield more time control. Perhaps most of these reasons are encapsuled by the anonymous author of "Functions of an Executive":

As nearly everyone knows, an executive has practically nothing to do except:

decide what is to be done;

tell somebody to do it;

listen to reasons why it should not be done, why it should be done by someone else, or why it should be done in a different way;

follow up to see if the thing has been done;

discover it has not been done;

inquire why it has not been done;

listen to excuses from the person who should have done it;

follow up again to see if the thing has been done, only to discover it has been done incorrectly;

point out how it should have been done;

conclude that as long as it has been done it might as well be left where it is;

consider how much simpler and better the thing would have been done if he had done it himself; and

> reflect sadly that he could have done it right in 20
> minutes, but instead had to spend 2 days to find out
> why it took 3 weeks for somebody else to do it wrong.[6]

Probably every manager feels some of these frustrations from time to time. Although clear instructions and explicit expectations won't cure all of the ills described, they can minimize those problems. How a manager delegates can make a big difference in the results obtained.

Delegation is not simply a "go/no go" situation. A manager can delegate in a variety of ways, depending on the importance and urgency of a project and the ability of the person to whom the manager is delegating. For instance, a manager can delegate a task in any of the following ways:

- "Look into this matter and bring me all the facts you can get on it."
- "Look into this matter, let me know if you think there is problem that should be worked on, and if so, give me prioritized list of alternatives that are available to us."
- "Look into this, let me know what, if anything, should done about it by memo, and do it unless I say not to."
- "Take action on this matter and keep me informed o results."

Effectiveness in delegation depends on the content work delegated and the manner in which it is done. Ross V of Wharton's School of Finance and Commerce, has prov following three guidelines for managers to use in whether to delegate a particular project or activity believes that managers should:

1. retain those projects or activities on which they I information or more expertise than any subordina
2. retain those activities that will require change practices, but delegate those that are primari with maintaining stability; and

3. delegate those activities or projects that primarily involve responding to the requests of others for more information.[7]

Delegation is not some gimmick a manager can use for unloading undesirable work on subordinates in order to have time to work on other matters. It takes time to do it right. It may take a lot of counseling and coaching before others learn to do things the way the manager likes them done. However, delegation can be an effective tool for both controlling the time and increasing overall effectiveness.

## CREATING TIME-CONSCIOUS HABITS

Many time-saving techniques amount to little more than commonsense managerial practices. What is involved is changing some habitual ways of doing things. Habits, however, are not easy to change, as most people who have made New Year's resolutions have found. Habits have a tremendous gravity pull, and changing them requires more than will power and minor tinkering. In order to change existing habits, a manager should do the following:

- Write down what specific changes are desired and what new way of operating is preferred.
- Decide how important the new way is. Count the costs.
- Share both your objective and commitment with other people at work.
- Allow no deviation from your plan of action during the first few weeks.
- Find some way to reward yourself for progress on a regular basis.

These steps can aid in developing habits that save time. In developing plans for saving time, there is a wide range of possible actions a manager can take. Some of these include the following:

1. *Set the deadlines for every project.* Even if a project doesn't have a deadline, setting one can get the work done and out of the way. This prevents procrastination or spending too much time on it.

2. *Visit the offices of others.* When a manager visits the office of someone else, he is more in control of how long the discussion will last.

3. *Speed up the mail.* Answering interoffice memos or passing along information on a letter by writing in longhand on the face of the correspondence can save time and the expense of typing a separate response.

4. *Cut the flow of the in-basket.* A secretary can screen junk mail and underline key points in trade journal articles in order to allow the manager to skim such material for any relevance to the work.

5. *Use idle time.* Try to have something that can be worked on while waiting for others, travelling, or the like.

6. *Use a reminder system.* Tickler files and regular "to do" lists can improve personal organization.

7. *Set time limits.* Meetings, interviews, and conferences can go on and on unless there are explicit time limits established before they begin.

8. *Decline nonessential obligations.* It is important to say "No, I'm sorry; even though I'd like to do that, I just don't have the time" to attractive offers that will make little difference in your job.

9. *Assess the use of your time.* Asking yourself regularly "Is what I'm doing the best use of my time?" can be a good reminder to focus on what counts.

10. *Be flexible.*

Saving even a few minutes each day can have an impact. Ten minutes saved each day will net a full, productive week each year. In an average lifetime, it means one more year of useful activity.

## SUMMARY

Time is a valuable resource, and unless *it* is managed well, nothing else can be. It is a unique resource, but one that is talked about more than it is controlled. As Lord Chesterfield so aptly put it, "There is nothing which I wish more that you should know than the true use and value of time. It is in everybody's mouth, but in few people's practice." Chesterfield was well aware of how easy it is to talk about controlling time use, but how difficult it is to actually do it. Walter Scott, writing in 1811, noted that the demands on managers in particular are so plentiful that a manager "is exhausted no more by his actual achievements than by the things which he is compelled to resist doing." No doubt the demands on a manager's time have increased several-fold since Scott's day.

In fact, management professor Curtis Jones believes that the minimization of demands on a manager's time deserves almost as much attention as is now devoted to profit maximization. Increasingly in making a business decision, return on time invested is as important a criterion as return on capital invested. Jones believes that a case can be made for the allegation that saving managerial time is one of the largest "industries" in the country. After all, it employs more than ten million clerks, bookkeepers, and secretaries whose primary function is to gather information, process it, and then disseminate it again for the manager.

Many managers have tried half a dozen or more ways to use their time more effectively. Some of these things no doubt help, at least for a while. Managing time can be elusive, especially when a manager has so many conflicting time demands. However, this is partly the nature of managerial work. It would be undesirable to become too streamlined or too time-conscious. However, most managers can make some changes in their daily routines that will make them both more efficient and more effective. A manager must strive to attain each of these goals.

## REFERENCES

1. Stephen R. Covey, *How to Succeed with People.* Salt Lake City: Deseret Book, 1971, p. 97.

2.  Sune Carlson, *Executive Behavior: A Study of the Workload and the Working Methods of Managing Directors.* Stockholm: Stromberg, 1951, p. 21.

3.  Peter Drucker, *The Effective Executive.* New York: Harper & Row, 1967.

4.  Joseph M. Trickett, "A More Effective Use of Time," *California Management Review.* Vol. IV, 1962, pp. 3–7.

5.  Robert Townsend, *Up the Organization.* New York: Alfred A. Knopf, 1970.

6.  Cited in R. Alec Mackenzie, *The Time Trap.* New York: McGraw-Hill, 1975.

7.  Ross A. Webber, *Time and Management.* New York: Van Nostrand Reinhold, 1972.

# CHAPTER II
# THE CHALLENGE
# OF MANAGING

To manage is to bring about, to cause to happen, to have responsibility for, or to accomplish. To manage is also to set a course and to take action, not simply to sit back and respond to events as they occur. Managing involves both action and reflection in those arenas the manager chooses to enter. Without making such choices, managerial work degenerates into custodial activities only. For many people in managerial positions, determining courses of action for significant issues and then pursuing them is a major challenge. Several years after being installed as the president of the University of Cincinnati, Warren Bennis described what he saw as an "unconscious conspiracy" of well-meaning subordinates to prevent him from being an effective manager:

I had become the victim of an amorphous, unintentional conspiracy to prevent me from doing anything whatever to change the university's status quo. Even those of my associates who fully shared my hopes to set new goals and work toward creative change were unconsciously doing the most to insure that I would never find the time to begin. People play the old Army game. They do not want to take responsibility for or bear the consequences of decisions that they should properly make. Everybody dumps his "wet babies" on my desk even though I have neither the diapers nor the information to take care of them.[1]

This is a common problem faced by many managers: How can the time be found to do the things that *must* be done and still have time to do the other creative and innovative things that *should* be done? Balancing the "musts" and "shoulds" may not be easy, but a good balance is necessary. The lack of an appropriate balance between the "musts" and "shoulds" will, moreover, spell failure even for the most conscientious manager.

## PATTERN OF FAILURE

Ineffective managers seem to approach their work in ways very different from those of effective managers. Their actions follow a predictable pattern that keeps them from improving their effectiveness. One common tendency in this regard is the proclivity to operate by "gut feeling." Often, a manager will simply "feel" that the basis of a problem is such-and-such, or reject a problem's solution as unworkable because "I don't think it would be accepted by these people." Although a manager should not totally ignore either hunches or intuition, they should be checked out to see how accurate they are. Especially in the matter of knowing employee attitudes or feelings, there is a considerable body of evidence suggesting that managers are not very intuitive or knowledgeable.[2]

A second issue that contributes to poor managerial performance is inappropriate attention to detail. Not getting involved in the details of the work leaves managers at the mercy of other people's judgment in matters where they should be making decisions and providing direction. In-depth knowledge can supply managers not only with valuable information but also with confidence that they are pursuing a well-thought-out course of action.

A third factor suggestive of an ineffective manager is an inability to accurately gauge priorities. Ultimately, some things are more important than others. Some deadlines can be extended, while others had better be met. If a manager's time is ruled only on the basis of what must be done next, coming to grips with the central demands of the job will probably never occur.

A fourth element that contributes to an overall pattern of failure is an inability to assume responsibility for others. As manager, a person automatically accepts the obligation to serve both the subordinates and the customers to whom the unit provides a product or service. Implicitly, both parties are promised a satisfactory relationship. Managing these dual relationships is demanding.

Sometimes a competent professional fails to make an adequate transition to manager because being responsible for the output of others feels uncomfortable. What makes it possible for some people to make this transition to manager so easily? By and large, it seems that confidence in their personal ability and judgment makes it possible for them to accept their subordinates' legitimate dependence needs and to adjust to the responsibility of being accountable for the output of others.

A fifth element that contributes to managerial failure is not dealing appropriately with problem employees. In some offices, elaborate dynamics develop for dealing with these problems. Conspiracies to hide the truth can grow up around people who don't perform. In such situations, people are eased into impotence under the guise of kindness. If they are terminated, they may be genuinely shocked. "No one complained about my work" is as likely to be the truth as a defensive reaction; they simply may not have been told that their work was substandard. The same manager who can make a multimillion-dollar decision on where to purchase raw materials for a new plant may go to great lengths to avoid confronting an employee and working through any performance problems.

Finally, a sixth practice that indicates poor managerial ability is simply not knowing—and not learning—what contributes to managerial effectiveness and what detracts from it. Those who manage badly are often unaware that they are alienating fellow employees. In other cases, they may realize that things could be improved, but they do not have the knowledge or skills to take appropriate action. Their own lack of awareness limits their ability to achieve desired results.

## PROFILE OF SUCCESS

Managing is tremendously difficult at every level of an organization. No single approach will work every time. People are different and situations vary, and because of this a manager must be flexible enough to adapt appropriately. This is a big order that is not easily accomplished, but it is fundamental to management success.

While effective managers are flexible and versatile, ineffective managers are just the opposite. Their experience has taught them to approach various problems in certain ways, and they see no reason to modify or adjust these basic approaches. However, the orientations that worked so well in the past may now be a liability. One or two essential ingredients may have changed in the current circumstance that make the past approach inappropriate. Effective managers use a number of tools and techniques that are selected after carefully analyzing the pertinent conditions in the problematic situation.

Careful analysis causes a manager to be well attuned to the demands and constraints inherent in a particular situation. While this may be done in a management training course or at the insistence of a superior on a particular project, it is usually neglected in routine practices and decisions. The unrelenting pace at which managers work often inhibits them from performing the careful analysis of situations that should be scrutinized.

The pace of managerial work makes time a critical resource to manage well. Since managers assume responsibility for others and their output, they must be available when subordinates need their direction or support. If they are inaccessible or unapproachable, their effectiveness will be impaired. In addition, since they must manage the boundary relationships between their groups and certain outside people, they must be responsive to the needs and demands of those others, as well.

A manager is judged by both subordinates and superiors for the ability to manage the multiple relationships inherent in the job. If the manager seems only to "look upward," both obtaining and maintaining the loyalty of subordinates will be difficult. At the same time, unless the subordinates feel the manager has upward influence, effectively directing their activities will be equally hard.

Managers cope best with the conflicting expectations of their position when they recognize that the formal authority structure is only one aspect of an organization. The informal social exchanges that occur between people at work are at least as important as the more formal relationships. Fritz Roethlisberger, former professor at the Harvard Business School, described the relationship between the formal and informal aspects of an organization and gave some tips on how to manage each in a classic article published in 1945:

> In business (and in unions too) there are not only "men of goodwill" but also men with extraordinary skill in the direction of securing cooperative effort. These men, at all levels, perform an "administrative" function, the importance of which is too little recognized. Much of their time is spent in facilitating the process of communication and in gaining the wholehearted cooperation of men. Many of them are not too logically articulate, but they have appreciation for a point of view different from their own. Not only can they appreciate the fact that a person can be different from themselves but, more important still, they can accept his right to be different. They always seem to have the time to listen to the problems and difficulties of the others. They do not pose as "experts;" they know when to secure the appropriate aid from others.

Such "administrators," selfless and sometimes acting in a way which appears to be lacking in ambition, understand the importance of achieving group solidarity—the importance of "getting along," rather than of "getting ahead." They take personal responsibility for the mixed situations, both technical and human, that they administer. They see to it that the newcomer has an effective and happy relationship with his fellow workers, as well as getting the work out. Accomplishing their results through leisurely social interaction rather than vigorous formal action, more interested in getting their human relationships straight than in getting their words and logics straight, more interested in being "friendly" to their fellow men than in being abstractly "fair," and never allowing their paperwork to interfere with this process of friendliness, they offer a healthy antidote to the formal logics of the modern factory organization previously described.[3]

Roethlisberger was saying more than that managerial effectiveness required "good communications" or "good human relationships." He was instead pointing out some of the dilemmas managers face in trying to do their work and offering some personal insights on how to manage the informal aspects of an organization. These insights, gleaned from his own analysis and observation, were the results of a behavioral scientist trying to understand how people work together best in an organizational context.

## BEHAVIORAL SCIENCE AND THE MANAGER'S ROLE

The findings of behavioral science point to ways in which the manager can do a better job. Research has suggested some very specific things that both aid and hinder managerial effectiveness. However, management is and probably always will be an art because it depends so heavily on intuitive judgments.

But management is still also part science. To be effective, a manager must be both analytical and perceptive. Unfortunately, some people have confused the findings of behavioral science research with advanced personal theories of action that are based on questionable assumptions. James Clark, professor of Management at UCLA, has catalogued some of the more important findings of behavioral science research and the distortions some people have advanced that others believe. It seems that in this area as well as others "a little knowledge is a dangerous thing." In the following table is a list of statements that are supported by research, followed by some of the oversimplified or distorted versions. Since the confusion occurs on various topics, they are grouped accordingly.

### Managerial Research: Findings and Distortions

| Finding | Distortion |
| --- | --- |
| *Organizational Behavior* | |
| Knowledge exists about organizational behavior. | If you know enough, you can solve any administrative problem. |
| There are nonlogical personality aspects that powerfully affect what people do. | People are basically illogical. |
| People's behavior is partially influenced by social factors. | People's behavior is determined by group memberships. |
| People's work aspirations have many aspects: self-esteem, friendship, economic security, status, and so on. | Pay—especially incentive pay—isn't of much importance any more. |
| People perform better if they feel respected and valued by their supervisors. | Giving employees whatever they want makes them perform better. |
| *Cooperation and Conflict* | |
| A way of thinking about differences between people affords a better position to manage them appropriately. | You should always get along with people and avoid any conflicts. |

| | |
|---|---|
| Shared goals encourage collaboration between groups of people. | Everyone must think alike in order to be able to work together. |

### Administration

| | |
|---|---|
| Effective managers identify problem areas and gauge the performance of their units. | Managers should study situations and act on them only after hours of deliberation. |
| Effective managers think of an organization as both a formal, technical system and an informal, social system. | You almost have to be a behavioral scientist to be a good manager. |
| Getting people together to explore a problem can sometimes result in a good solution. | Getting people together in a group to talk about their problems will solve all of the problems. |
| Effective managers are flexible and adaptable to various situations. | Consistency of values is neither desirable nor useful. |
| Effective managers value people as individuals and not just as pairs of hands. | If you pay attention to human relations, you don't need to know about the business. |

It is unfortunately true that many managers and professors of management agree with at least half a dozen of the distortions. Perhaps the reason for this is that, in our haste to obtain simplified rules for action taking, we all tend to exaggerate a guideline to dramatize a point. In place of careful analysis and planned action, a person will too often rely on a slogan and a generalization. Effective management is not, however, so founded. Effective management is, instead, grounded in the ability of individuals to ask "why" and to make work experiences part of an on-going learning environment for themselves and others. After all, if a manager is not introspective regarding the work, learning from the job and passing this knowledge on to others will be difficult.

## SELF-STUDY QUESTIONS FOR MANAGERS

Ultimately, managerial effectiveness is improved by assessing the methods for doing various activities and altering those that are inefficient. This means that from time to time managers must consciously ask themselves if they are actually managing as well as they are able. At such times they must detach themselves from the content of the work in order to analyze the work's general procedures. This is not easy to do, but it is an important task. Moreover, research seems to indicate that most managers do not learn or develop new ideas from their work-related experiences. They may again try a solution that worked for them once, but seldom do managers attempt to catalogue their experiences or ask what can be learned about managing from past experiences.

One way for managers to better learn from the job is to compile a list of questions to be asked that will assess their managerial performance. Of course, this requires a certain amount of objectivity and detachment. However, since managers will conduct this review exclusively for their own benefit, there is no reason why they should not be accurate. Inflated answers to self-study questions hurt no one but themselves.

Any manager can design questions that are appropriate for personal developmental goals. A list of possible self-study questions are offered below. In answering these questions, or any others that focus on assessing managerial work, it is useful to test the answers by asking two additional questions: "How do I know?" and "So what?" If a manager is satisfied after employing these two extra criteria, the self-assessment has probably been rigorous.

Here for review are some self-study questions for assessing managerial performance.

### The informational function

- Where do I get most of my information? Do I rely too heavily on one source?
- Do I try to get important information from first-hand sources?

- Do I spend time observing various operations, just talking to people, and noticing how things are done in order to feel the organizational pulse?
- Do I keep people who report to me informed enough so that they can take action on routine matters?
- How do I know that the methods I use for disseminating information to various parts of the organization actually get the message through?
- How do I know that a project is being worked on satisfactorily? Do I provide direction without being overbearing?

### The interpersonal function

- What would the initial reaction of specific subordinates be if I requested a meeting in my office in ten minutes? Would they be concerned? suspicious? apprehensive? interested?
- Are differences welcomed as a natural part of organizational arrangements or are they shunned and suppressed?
- When differences arise, do I resist resolving them until I first understand why they exist?
- Do I communicate high performance standards to others by the actions I take as well as by the words I use?
- Do employees have opportunities to be challenged and to feel responsible for the work they do?
- Is good performance actually rewarded? Can employees see that good performance results in more money, status, recognition, or positive feedback?

### The decisional function

- Do I have a system for locating opportunities and identifying problems that require my attention?
- In problem solving, do I consider what a person with a frame of reference totally opposite my own would say about the way I have gathered information, defined desired outcomes,

and formulated a problem statement as a test of my thinking?

- What method do I have for deciding who should be involved in making particular decisions?
- Do I consciously attempt to control my time through my work schedule?
- Do I have a clear idea of which activities will give me a good return for my time if I invest energy in them?
- Am I continually trying to form habits that will make me more effective?

## SUMMARY

The manager's job is vital to society. The nature of nearly every creative effort and of every institution requires the administrative and interpersonal skills of effective managers. However, such skills do not automatically appear after the individual's appointment to a managerial position. In fact, a person may know a lot about management as a body of knowledge and still be an ineffective manager. There is an important difference between knowing about management and having the skills, the self-concept, the confidence, and the commitment to perform managerial work well.

People can develop the skills and orientations necessary to manage effectively through continual observation, analysis, and practice. Managing is not a static activity; it is dynamic and requires both vision and alertness. Managers must be able to articulate the purpose behind various actions and be sensitive to their ramifications when implemented. If so, they will be equal to the challenge of managing.

## REFERENCES

1. Warren Bennis, *The Unconscious Conspiracy*. New York: Amacon, 1976. p. 19.
2. Alfred J. Marrow, David G. Bowers, and Stanley E. Seashore, *Management By Participation*. New York: Harper & Row, 1967.

3. Fritz Roethlisberger, "The Foreman: Master and Victim of Double Talk," *Harvard Business Review*, March–April 1965, pp. 22–26. Although this article focuses on the foreman and not the manager, the role conflicts and ambiguities inherent in each position are similar.

4. The data in this list are adapted from James V. Clark, "Distortions of the Behavioral Sciences," *California Management Review*, Vol. 6, 1963, pp. 55–60.